Rousseau's *Émile*
and
Early Children's Literature

by

Sylvia W. Patterson

The Scarecrow Press, Inc.
Metuchen, N.J.   1971

Acknowledgments

The author sincerely appreciates the assistance given to her by Dr. James A. Preu of Florida State University and by Mr. John Shaw, Curator of the Shaw Collection of Childhood in Poetry, of the Florida State University Library, who inspired the writer by his love for children and their books.

A number of libraries were kind enough to lend or provide a copy of books from their rare book rooms. The writer gratefully acknowledges the cooperation of the libraries of the following universities: University of North Carolina for The Fairy Spectator; Columbia University, The Juvenile Tatler; Yale University, Anecdotes of a Boarding-School; Princeton University, "Introduction" to The Life and Perambulation of a Mouse and Original Stories from Real Life; Duke University, Thoughts on the Education of Daughters; University of Florida, Forgotten Tales of Long Ago; Harvard University, Cobwebs to Catch Flies; and the Shaw Collection of Florida State University for Evenings at Home and the second volume of Cobwebs to Catch Flies. The author also appreciates the Cleveland Public Library's sending E. V. Lucas's "Introduction" to Old-Fashioned Tales. Two members of the Strozier Library at Florida State University deserve special recognition for requesting all of the above books--Mrs. Ilona Turrisi and Mrs. Bobbie Johnson.

The author also wishes to thank her friends Dr. Barbara Ewell and Mrs. Dianne Mellon for giving unselfishly of their time; and to her friend Dr. Paul T. Nolan of the University of Southwestern Louisiana, the author acknowledges a long-standing debt and wishes to express her sincere appreciation of his advice and his friendship.

Finally, the author recognizes her debt to her husband for his patience and helpful suggestions and to her parents for their moral support. She dedicates this study to Billy.

Table of Contents

		Page
Acknowledgments		iii

Chapter

I.	Introduction	7
	Summary of _Emile_	15
II.	Anna Laetitia Barbauld and John Aikin	40
	Lessons for Children	42
	Hymns in Prose for Children	47
	Evenings at Home	50
III.	Thomas Day	62
	The History of Sandford and Merton	64
	The History of Little Jack	73
IV.	Maria Edgeworth	79
	Early Lessons	81
	The Parent's Assistant	83
	Moral Tales	88
V.	Mary Wollstonecraft	101
	Original Stories from Real Life	104
VI.	Lady Eleanor Fenn, "The Kilner Sisters"	114
	Cobwebs to Catch Flies	115
	The Fairy Spectator	118
	The Juvenile Tatler	121
	The Life and Perambulation of a Mouse	124
	Anecdotes of a Boarding-School	128
	The Village School	131
	Jemima Placid	133
	The Adventures of a Pincushion	135

Memoirs of a Peg-Top   137

VII   Hannah More and Sarah Trimmer   143

       Cheap Repository Tracts   145
       An Easy Introduction to the Knowledge
          of Nature   147
       Fabulous Histories, or The History of
          the Robins   151

VIII   Conclusions   158

Bibliography   163

Index   173

Chapter I

Introduction

Almost all histories of children's literature in
England mention the impact of the writings of Jean Jacques
Rousseau, especially Emile, which was published in France
in 1762 and first translated into English the same year. [1]
Emile arrived at a time when children's literature was in
its infancy. John Newbery, the first publisher to be interested in works written especially for children, had begun
his illustrious career in 1744 in London. By the time of
his death in 1767, and primarily through his efforts, the
foundation for children's literature (that is, books written
to be read by children) had been laid. Before Emile, most
of the authors in this area were anonymous; Sarah Fielding
in her work The Governess (1749) is the primary exception
to the rule of anonymity. Before Emile many of the books
were merely children's versions of adult books, such as
Pilgrim's Progress, Gulliver's Travels, and Robinson
Crusoe. [2] After Emile, this trend changed, and the movement of writing expressly for children gained impetus. It
is the purpose of this study to consider the influence of
Rousseau's Emile, and to determine the extent of the influence of this work upon the major writers of children's
literature in England in the late eighteenth century. Both
positive and negative influences are considered; that is,
both those works which agree with Rousseau's ideas and
those which were written in opposition to them are included.

The literary historians agree that Rousseau's influence is extensive, although they do not all treat the subject
with the same degree of thoroughness. Some historians of
children's literature, such as Florence V. Barry (A Century
of Children's Books), Cornelia L. Meigs (A Critical
History of Children's Literature), and Montrose J. Moses
(Children's Books and Reading), devote whole chapters to
Rousseau's influence; but they consider only major works.
They do not treat negative effects or the writers who were
only slightly influenced. Others, such as F. J. Harvey
Darton (Children's Books in England), Dorothy Gardiner

(English Girlhood at School), Paul Hazard (<u>Books, Children,</u>
<u>and Men</u>), and May H. Arbuthnot (<u>Children and Books</u>),
make only broad general references to the impact of <u>Emile</u>.
Between these two treatments stand M. F. Thwaite (<u>From</u>
<u>Primer to Pleasure</u>) and Bess P. Adams (<u>About Books and</u>
<u>Children</u>). Moses, for example, says of Rousseau:

> He opened the way for a self-conscious striving
> on the part of authors to meet the demands of a
> child's nature by furnishing the best literary
> diet--according to educational theories--for juvenile
> minds. 3

Harvey Darton claims:

> There can be no doubt whatever that in the
> period immediately after Newbery's death [1767],
> the works of Rousseau had a very direct effect
> upon English books for children. Many writers
> acknowledge their debt to <u>Emile</u>. 4

Unfortunately, Darton does not elaborate.

      May H. Arbuthnot does not give Rousseau as much
credit as Darton does: "The only thing these writers
seemed to have carried over from Rousseau was the idea
of following the child's natural interests and developing
these. "5   M. F. Thwaite calls Rousseau's influence on
educational theory and practice and on books written for
children "tremendous";6   and she credits him, along with
other Romantic writers who followed him, with giving a
new theme to children's books: the appreciation of the
wonders of nature. 7   Cornelia Meigs calls Rousseau's
impact "both curious and unexpected, "8 and Elva S. Smith
in her syllabus of the history of children's literature makes
the following statement:

> Books for children in the late 18th and early 19th
> centuries show the influence of Rousseau to such
> an extent that a knowledge of his educational
> theories is fundamental [to any study of the his-
> tory of children's literature]. 9

      While most of these critics recognize some debt to
Rousseau, they are not always consistent in praising
Rousseau for his influence.   Florence V. Barry claims
that "Rousseau taught two generations of writers to

substitute living examples for maxims";[10] but at the same
time she claims the "the great writers were neither Lilliputian
nor Rousseauist."[11] Other writers object to Rousseau's
views on the inferiority of women, on the age at which reason
is acquired or developed, and on the age at which children
should be permitted to read books, and on other points.

Some historians credit Rousseau with definite contributions,
such as the stock literary character of the teacher
who knows all and is always available to turn all experiences
into significant and never insipid lessons,[12] the device of
children learning through actual experiences,[13] and the philosophy
of recognizing the child as a child, not as a miniature
adult.[14] According to R. H. Eliassen, Rousseau can be
credited for his negative education idea--the child is taught
virtue by not being exposed to vice, his idea of punishment
suited to the crime, and his idea of instilling the desire to
learn, making the child wish to educate himself.[15] Though
all the writers who discuss Rousseau recognize the influence
of Emile on children's literature, they do not treat the subject
in a comprehensive manner and such a study is essential
to understanding the history of children's books in the
late eighteenth century. It was, after all, that period which
led directly to the great period of children's literature--the
nineteenth century. This study traces the influence of Emile
on the major writers of children's literature in that period
in a more comprehensive manner, and includes more authors
than any other study, with the aim of determining just how
extensive Rousseau's influence was.

Listed below are the major writers of children's
books between 1763 and 1800[16] who are considered in this
study. Also listed are the works for which those writers
are best known. Selections which seem most typical will
be made from some of the longer works. John Aikin and
his sister Anna Laetitia Barbauld, Evenings at Home (1792-
1796); Anna Laetitia Barbauld, Lessons for Children (1780)
and Hymns in Prose for Children (1781); Thomas Day, The
History of Sandford and Merton (1783, 1786, 1789) and The
History of Little Jack (1788); Maria Edgeworth, The Parent's
Assistant (1796), Moral Tales (1800), and Early Lessons
(1801); Lady Eleanor Fenn, The Fairy Spectator (1789); The
Juvenile Tatler (1789), and Cobwebs to Catch Flies (1783?);
Dorothy Kilner, Anecdotes of a Boarding-School, The Life
and Perambulation of a Mouse, The Village School; and her
sister, Mary Jane Kilner, Memoirs of a Peg-Top, The Adventures
of a Pincushion, Jemima Placid (1788);[17] Hannah

More, Cheap Repository Tracts (1795-1798); Sarah Trimmer,
An Easy Introduction to the Knowledge of Nature (1780) and
Fabulous Histories (1786)--later called The History of the
Robins; and Mary Wollstonecraft, Original Stories from Real
Life (1788).

    Furthermore, the following works, although not writ-
ten for children, explain their authors' positions and educational beliefs; consequently, they will be used to determine
their authors' familiarity with Rousseau's ideas: Richard
and Maria Edgeworth, Practical Education (1797); Hannah
More, Strictures on the Modern System of Female Education (1801); Mary Wollstonecraft, Thoughts on the Education
of Daughters (1787); Anna Laetitia Barbauld's On Education;
and John Aikin, On the Imitative Principle.

    To study the influence of Emile on these writers ne-
cessitates a definition of influence.   It is this author's intention to show what Rousseau's ideas were, that these writers
had knowledge of them, and that some of these ideas appear
in their works.   It is important to note, however, that some
of Rousseau's ideas were not original; in many cases his
main contribution was the popularization of certain ideas in
the air at the time.   Thus it can be shown only that Rousseau probably was the source for some of the theories of
education which shaped children's literature of the period;
circumstantial evidence will have to stand where absolute
proof cannot be provided, but circumstantial evidence can
often be quite convincing.

    In order to study the major ideas of Emile and their
relationship to children's literature, it is essential to devote
some space to Emile and to the major problems about which
critics and readers have long complained.   This introduction
to Emile, then, will consist of four sections: Rousseau's
educational works, originality and contradiction or paradox
in Emile, the reception and popularity of Emile in the eighteenth century, and a summary of the main ideas of Emile
which influenced children's literature.

    Emile was written between 1757 and 1760 and pub-
lished in 1762 in France when its author was fifty years old.
Rousseau's ideas on education had been taking shape for
some time before 1757.   In fact, one critic of Emile claims
that Rousseau's ideas were born as a result of his experience as a school master in 1740 and 1743 from which he
compiled his Projet d'éducation de M. de Sainte-Marie.[18]

By 1757, Rousseau had also completed La Nouvelle Héloïse, in which he pictures a family group living close to Nature; at this time he began to consider an education based on the child's being close to Nature. It is in this work that Rousseau pictures the perfect woman--Julie; she is the mouthpiece for his educational ideas in Part V, Letter 3. According to Leonora B. Lang:

> Julie's method of teaching her children contains the germ of what was developed later in Emile; but in the four years that elapsed between the two books, Rousseau's views had made a great stride. [19]

Any reading of the two works would certainly support Mrs. Lang's statement. William Boyd claims the ideas in Emile also appear in the minor educational writings, including La Nouvelle Héloïse. [20] His claim is true; but at the same time, a more significant point is that Emile is clearly the most comprehensive statement of Rousseau's educational ideas.

In addition to the two works mentioned above, Rousseau discussed his views on education in a letter to the Duke of Wurtemberg dated November 16, 1763. Fully a year after Emile was published, Rousseau went into some detail about the education of women, particularly about the choice of a governess. The educational works, which followed Emile and the letters to the Duke of Wurtemberg, were numerous. Most were letters to various people (Madame de Roquin, Abbé M., Madame de T.); in addition to the letters were Considerations on the Government of Poland (in which he discusses education in Chapter IV), and, of course, The Confessions.

There is also one other work which deserves mention here, although it is not an educational work. It is Emile et Sophie ou les solitaires, an unfinished sequel to Emile, begun shortly after 1762 but not published until 1780. Epistolary in style, it consists of only one finished letter and one unfinished. In it, Emile and Sophie have grown apart after suffering hardships, and Sophie claims to be pregnant by another man. Emile leaves home and is eventually made a slave. There seems to be little doubt that Rousseau meant an eventual reunion of Sophie and Emile at which time Sophie's name would be cleared; and Rousseau would have shown the survival of his pupil under circumstances which would have crushed a lesser man.

Two of the main points which evoked criticism of
<u>Emile</u> are its originality or lack of it and the contradictions
or paradoxes of the work. Both will be discussed briefly,
but neither limited the influence of <u>Emile</u> in the eighteenth
century as the following discussion will show. Much of what
Rousseau wrote in <u>Emile</u> was not original. A comparison
with Locke's ideas shows that the two did not differ widely.
For the most part, Rousseau merely went further than Locke.
Both men believed in physical development along with intellectual development. Both emphasized ability to reason and
teaching of subjects useful in later life; both were for con-
structive teaching, showing the right way rather than the
wrong way; both felt knowledge should be combined with
pleasure. [21] Locke and Rousseau were both instrumental in
proving the child's mind is different from that of his elders.
Rousseau himself in <u>Emile</u> acknowledges his indebtedness to
many writers, among them Locke, Buffon, and Montaigne.
James P. Munroe recognizes Rousseau's lack of originality
also. In fact, he goes so far as to say:

> [Emile] contains scarcely an idea that is not al-
> ready in the Greek and Latin literatures, in
> Rabelais, Montaigne, or Locke. Whole passages,
> even, if we put faith in his detractors, are taken
> bodily from obscurer writings. [22]

Green takes a different position; he claims that Rousseau
was influenced by Plato, Saint Augustine, Fénelon, Le Père
Lamy, and the Oratorians, in addition to Montaigne and
Locke. Nevertheless, he says: "In the opinion of all modern educationists these borrowings only serve to underline
the originality of <u>Emile</u>."[23] Compayré agrees with Green,
for he feels that Rousseau's educational ideas are so original that "they still have claims to novelty."[24] The truth of
the matter appears to lie somewhere in between. Rousseau
had the ability to popularize ideas which were not originally
his. Warner suggests that the basis of Rousseau's appeal
in eighteenth-century England was his sentimentality.[25] Indeed, it was this quality which gave Rousseau's works their
popular appeal, not the quality of originality or the lack of
it.

In turning to the problem of contradiction or paradox
in <u>Emile</u>, most readers will clearly see why this issue a-
rose: there are numerous contradictions. The child, for
example, will hardly know what a book is at twelve (80),[26]
yet Rousseau believes Emile will know how to read before

he is ten (81).[27] Fables and maxims are not good for use
as examples by which to teach, but the example of a perfect
parent or tutor is good.[28] The tutor should tell the child
the truth and punish lying; yet the tutor practices all kinds
of deceit in his contriving to bring about various experiences
for his pupil. One example of deceit is the tutor's pretending to be lost so that the child can use his astronomy lesson
of the previous day to find the way home (143-44). A list of
deceits on the part of the tutor would be quite lengthy. It
will suffice to say that perhaps the final and most crushing
contradiction occurs at the very close of the book where
Emile is on his own--grown and married, and supposedly
independent. He claims that he will need his tutor now more
than ever. If he is to be believed, Rousseau has failed at
one of his primary objectives: making Emile dependent on
no man or even on Lady Fortune.

        Contradictions with other works of Rousseau appear,
according to Archer. For a man so concerned with citizenship as to write Du Contrat Social, Rousseau appears to contradict this interest in citizenship by having Emile isolated
from society. For a man who is so intent upon picturing the
values of family life in La Nouvelle Héloïse, Rousseau seems
inconsistent when he has Emile removed from family life for
his first twenty years. The third apparent contradiction that
Archer finds is that of negative education, or teaching virtue
by not allowing the child to be exposed to vice.[29] The first
two seemingly arise from the paradox that man is born good,
yet he is everywhere corrupt and from the paradox of isola-
ting the child in order to prepare him for society. The
third seems clearly paradoxical in that the best teacher is he
who teaches least. An answer to the problem of isolation is
that clearly Rousseau did not expect his readers to take his
romantic setting literally. In the "Preface" Rousseau points
out the fact that Emile is only a model. Boyd claims, and
surely no one would disagree with his point, that Rousseau
chose a romantic setting for the opportunity it provided to
present effectively his ideas in the first person.[30] The
other paradoxes.are not so easily reconciled.

        Granting then the lack of originality in some cases
and the various paradoxes, wherein does the greatness of
Emile lie? Compayré claims it is "the paradoxical audacity
of its ideas" along with "the inspired and prophetic character
of its style" that make Emile great.[31] Henri Roddier answers: "Le triomphe de l'Emile consiste à pénétrer l'enfant
de religiosité et de morale par la seule vertu d'un contact

permanent avec la Nature."[32]   James P. Munroe, who accuses Rousseau of hardly an original word, answers:

> But Rousseau went farther than to stimulate vague
> yearnings. He proved that virtue springs from
> liberty and is, in its turn, the parent of liberty,
> of the only real freedom that man knows. . . .
> Others had preached, and would continue to preach,
> the rights of man; some, even at that early day,
> had proclaimed the rights of women; Rousseau
> championed the rights of the child,--the right to
> his mother's breast, the right to his father's guid-
> ance, the right to a home, the right to free physi-
> cal and mental development, the right to innocence,
> the right, finally, to be happy.[33]

One more definition of Emile's greatness is that of Lord
Morley, who says of Emile:

> It touched the deeper things of character. It
> filled parents with a sense of dignity and moment
> of their task. It cleared away the accumulation of
> clogging prejudices and obscure inveterate usage,
> which made education one of the dark formalistic
> arts. It admitted floods of light and air into the
> tightly closed nurseries and schoolrooms. It ef-
> fected the substitution of growth for mechanism.
> A strong current of manliness, wholesomeness,
> simplicity, self-reliance, was sent by it through
> Europe, while its eloquence was the most power-
> ful adjuration ever addressed to parental affection
> to cherish the young life in all love and consider-
> ate solicitude. It was the charter of youthful de-
> liverance.[34]

    The nineteenth and twentieth-century critics gave the
praise just cited; the eighteenth century reacted a little less
enthusiastically toward Emile. Emile was widely received
in England, for its author was already known from the publication of La Nouvelle Héloïse in 1760; the official burning
of Emile and Rousseau's subsequent flight from Geneva as-
sured the book a wide audience. J. H. Warner, in his ar-
tical, "Emile in Eighteenth-Century England," cites a study
made of some 218 private libraries of the period; Emile
ranked second of Rousseau's works in those libraries, and
fifteenth among all books in those libraries.[35] Yet works
on education often made no mention of Rousseau.[36] Well-

known writers in England mentioned Emile, however, as
various works and diaries and letters testify. Thomas
Gray, Mary Wollstonecraft, Horace Walpole, David Hume,
Thomas Day, the Edgeworths, James Beattie, William Godwin, John Wesley, Hannah More, William Blake, Edward
Gibbon, Joseph Warton, Edmund Burke, among others discussed Emile.[37] In spite of this wide reception, Warner
concludes that Emile's reputation was predominantly unfavorable.[38] Rousseau's character, his religion, and his attitude toward women account for some of the unpopularity.
An unfavorable reputation does not prevent a book from being influential, however, and as will be shown later, most
of the writers of children's books of the period read Emile
and reacted to it, one way or another.

Following are the principal ideas from Emile which
influenced the writers of children's books in the eighteenth
century. They are summarized by books with the first para-
graph of the five sections containing a summary of the main
ideas of that book.

Summary of Emile

Book I

On Education of Children Under Five

After a brief introduction, Rousseau discusses the
life of the child from his birth. He advocates breast feeding, fresh air, and loose clothing. He sees the natural
mother as the best nurse and the father as the best tutor
for the child. He recognizes the fact that the child learns
even at a very young age, and therefore that care should be
taken with his education from the very beginning.

All that God creates is good; it is man who corrupts.
An innocent child must be free from all corrupting influences
and independent of other men and their vices. This education comes from three sources: Nature, men, and things
(6). By Nature Rousseau means Nature within oneself; thus
education by Nature means allowing the child to develop
physically and psychologically on his own, allowing him to
be free.

The boy educated according to Rousseau will first
be a man (9), then a member of a trade or profession.
There will be no attempt to change his station in life; hence

he will always be in his right place (9). In the beginning of
his life, the infant should not be swaddled. After his entry
into this world, he is immediately wrapped in swaddling
bands and consequently deprived of his newborn freedom
(10). Then he is sent out to be nursed while his mother
resumes her gay daily pleasures in town; the truth is, he
needs his mother's love as much as he needs her milk. It
is true the woman who nurses him will come to love him in
time, but he needs love and affection before that time (10-
13).

Rousseau then states: "When women become good
mothers, men will be good husbands and fathers" (14). It
is the father's duty to educate his son, in addition to beget-
ting him and providing for him. As a mother with her love
is the child's best nurse, so is the father with his love the
child's best tutor (17).[39] Thus Rousseau is suggesting a
family circle which had long ceased to be customary, but
which appealed to many.

Rousseau does not describe the qualities of the tutor
in this volume to the extent that he does those of the governess in a letter to the Duke of Wurtemberg, dated November
16, 1763. Nevertheless, the tutor should be young and willing to devote a major part of his life to his student; for the
tutor will have complete control over the boy, and the two
must necessarily be almost inseparable. They may separate
by mutual consent only. When Rousseau develops his plan
further, it is easy to see why this condition is necessary.
The tutor must govern everything which happens to the child;
and the child must obey him. Both must love each other
for the plan to be successful. If they think they will soon
part, that love which is essential will not develop as it
should (20).

The child himself must also meet certain requirements. He cannot be sickly; for if he is, the tutor will
have to be more a sick nurse than a tutor. The body which
is feeble also makes for a feeble mind. Rousseau has very
little faith in medicine as a cure for the sick child and even
calls the art of medicine useless (23). To be sure, even if
the child is strong, he must have a good nurse in the absence of the best of all nurses, his own mother. He describes the diet of the nurse--which foods produce the best
milk (24-25). He also praises the fresh air of the country
over the foul city air (26). Rousseau then discusses bath-
ing the child, gradually reducing the heat of the water until

he can be bathed in ice cold water either in summer or winter.[40] Rousseau claims, and rightly so, that man's education begins at birth. It is the nurse, however, who seems to have the responsibility for teaching the very young infant. The child is to fear nothing. The nurse should show him things, carefully selected, so that he will be familiar with them and have no cause to fear them. Rousseau claims, in a most interesting example, that only these children who are brought up in houses free from spiders, fear spiders, often for their entire lives (30).

The language of the infant is the natural language common to all. While it is inarticulate, it has tone, stress, and meaning (32). The nurse should avoid excessive haste in teaching the child to speak. After all, the purpose of language is communication, and he can communicate. Rousseau is careful to distinguish between the crying resulting from needs and that resulting from whim. He warns the nurse to be careful not to sympathize with the child if she can do nothing to aid him except sympathize, lest the child learn to command the nurse (32-35). When the child does speak, the nurse should not correct his speech. He has a grammar of his own which is freer than the grammar of adults. If one always speaks correctly in front of him, he will learn to speak correctly without any overt correction, which may cause him to hesitate before he speaks and even cause him to stutter. The child should have certain words repeated to him, and the nurse should take care not to enlarge his vocabulary too soon, lest he use words whose meanings he does not fully understand (40).

Book II

On Education from Five to Twelve

It is in the period from five to twelve years old that the child makes great strides; yet he has not attained the age of reason. His education should be negative in regard to virtue and suited to his individual bent. He should learn never to hurt anyone. His physical development is of prime importance in this period of his education; the games which he learns develop him physically. The tutor should take care with regard to his sleep and his clothing, or lack of clothing. The child needs to develop his senses, including that sixth one--common sense.

By the age of five, the child must first learn courage

to bear slight ills. He should have liberty and fresh air,
and if he falls and hurts himself, that is good; for the small
pain will prepare him for the greater pains of life (41).
The child should be considered a child (44); as only half at
most of the children who are born will reach adulthood, the
tutor should not restrain the child too much and make his
early life miserable with only a promise of happiness in
adulthood--a state which he may likely not live to see (42-
43).

Rousseau next defines happiness as consisting of "de-
creasing the difference between our desires and our powers,
in establishing a perfect equilibrium between the power and
the will" (44). Then he claims that a man who is really
free desires only what he can do and thus can do all that he
desires. This equality of performance and desire, Rousseau
takes to be his fundamental maxim from which all his rules
of education spring (48). A child raised according to this
maxim will not be dependent upon others when he reaches
manhood. There are two kinds of dependence: on things
and on men; the latter is the work of society. Dependence
on things is non-moral according to Rousseau, so it is per-
missible; it is non-moral because it "does no injury to liberty and begets no vices." Dependence on men, however, gives
rise to all kinds of vice. It is to be avoided (49).

In regard to the problem of indulgence, Rousseau
states that the child should not have either to sit or run
just because his tutor feels he should. The tutor should see
that his own desires are free from caprice. At the same
time, the tutor should never answer a question or fulfill a
request that seems to arise from caprice on the part of the
child. But note that "children's caprices are never the work
of nature, but of bad discipline" (85). The child should not
learn empty phrases of politeness, such as "please," spoken
in the tone of a command (50). He should never be given
everything he wants, for he will grow accustomed to having
all he wants and will be miserable later when all such desires cannot possibly be fulfilled (51).

The tutor should not reason with the child; Locke,
whose theories were so popular, had said the tutor should.
Instead, the tutor is the master. At the same time, he is
not to order the child around, but to let him know only that
he, the child, is weak and the tutor is strong. The tutor
must be firm; Rousseau says: "Let your 'No,' once uttered,
be a wall of brass, against which the child may exhaust his

strength some five or six times, but in the end will try no
more to overthrow it" (55).

As tutor, give your pupil no lessons in words; he
must learn only from experience. Never punish him for the
sake of punishment alone. His heart is pure; there is no
original sin in it. Any damage he does is not wrong-doing
because wrong-doing depends upon harmful intent. According
to Rousseau: "If once he meant to do harm, his whole education would be ruined; he would be almost hopelessly bad"
(57).

Before the age of twelve, the child's education should
be merely negative; that is, he should not be taught virtue
or truth, but their opposites should be prevented from gain-
ing entry into the child's heart. From birth to twelve years
is the most dangerous period of life, for it is at that time
that errors and vices spring up (57). Let the child have
plenty of exercise, but let his mind remain idle as long as
possible (58). Most defects of body and mind come from the
same source: "the desire to make men of [children] before
their time" (91).

Learn the individual bent of the child in order to
know best how to teach him (58).[41] Do not be in a hurry.
The country is the best place to bring up children, for there
they are not likely to confront all kinds of passions and vice
(59). The country is a good place to teach them the important principle of property. Emile takes a corner of a garden and plants and cultivates some beans. He is very proud
of them; they "belong" to him. One day he finds that the
gardener has pulled them up. Upon being questioned, the
gardener explains that he had some Maltese melons there before Emile dug them up to plant beans. The two reach a
compromise, and Emile has learned through experience, not
through words, the idea of property (62-63).

The subject of lying comes up next. If a child lies,
his punishment should force him to see the consequences of
lying either by not being believed when he is telling the
truth or by being accused of something he has not done in
spite of his protests (65).

Locke would have the tutor also arrange it so that
when the child gives away something, he will get something
bigger in return. Rousseau disagrees completely, saying
such an action will make the child superficially generous,

but in reality, he will be greedy (67). Rousseau further
states that the only moral lesson suited for a child is:
"Never hurt anybody" (69). [42]

Rousseau does not agree with those who want to advance the prodigy beyond his years, for it is his belief that
before the age of reason, the child receives images, not i-
deas. He is very receptive to learning and can learn much
and even be able to repeat it, without being able to understand it. Therefore, children are incapable of judging, for
they have no true memory of ideas and relations. Learning
a second language before the age of fifteen is useless, for
although the child can memorize the words, the true acqui-
sition of language depends upon the ability to compare ideas
and the child cannot make the comparison. (In Book IV,
Rousseau claims that the learning of language is less useful
than one thinks: it will lead to a knowledge of grammar in
general, however (308).)

Rousseau then takes up other subjects of study, such
as geography, history, fables, and later geometry and astronomy. The child cannot see the relationship between a
map on a cardboard sphere and the paths of his father's es-
tate, thus geography is a poor subject for a child to study
when taught by the use of maps. History is also a poor subject for a child of this age because it is a collection of facts
and what is a fact to a child? The child cannot grasp anything beyond the present and knows little of the past (73-74).
(Rousseau has remarked earlier on the futility of telling a
child that something will be good or helpful in the future
when he has grown to manhood because he does not care
about a future time.)

To memorize a fable is useless, for merely learning
by heart does not insure understanding. In fact, fables often
cover the truth in such a way that the child may miss the
moral completely. Rousseau then cites La Fontaine's "The
Fox and the Crow" and shows why it is not suitable for teaching a child. In fact, he claims that the child will learn flat-
tery rather than the moral (77-80). Then Rousseau general-
izes and rejects all books as "the chief cause of [children's]
sorrows. Reading is the curse of childhood, yet it is almost the only occupation you can find for children" (80).
Reading will come later--age fifteen is early enough, and it
will come because Emile will want to learn to read. He
will not always be able to find someone to read his invitations to him; after a few are read too late for him to attend

the event, he will wish to read the next for himself (81).

In regard to the physical side of the child's life, the
tutor should let him wear bright colors for he likes them;
there is no need, however, to make him wear anything on
his head all year round. The tutor should not bundle him
up too much; it is the heat not the cold that is bad for him.
There are more infant deaths in August than any other time
(91-93). In fact, do not let the cold prevent him from going barefoot, but all broken glass should be removed first
(104).

Sleep is essential, but the child should not be accustomed to a particular bed; otherwise, he might find another
bed uncomfortable. He should be awakened sometimes so as
to accustom him to waking with a start. The child should
not become accustomed either to sleeping too long or to re-
lying upon another to awaken him (94-95).

The child should learn how to swim, for without that
knowledge he may drown. Too much concern is given to
learning to ride horseback; whereas the child's life will not
likely depend upon that ability (96). In addition to learning
to swim, the child should learn to use all his senses. If he
learns to use his sense of touch and hearing well, he should
have no trouble finding his way in the dark. In fact, he
should play games in the dark, so he will learn that there
is no reason to fear it (97-98).

The child should develop his senses so that he can
measure, perceive, and estimate distance (105). He should
learn to draw, not for art's sake, but to help him develop
an exactness of eye and a flexibility of hand (108). The pictures will be framed upon the walls: the worst ones in gilt
frames, the best in plain dark frames. The tutor will draw
with the child since the two are inseparable; he will be careful to progress as the child progresses and will, in fact, appear to be as unskillful as the child.[43]

Good games for children are the same as those for
men: tennis, billiards, archery, football. The playing of
musical instruments is also good. The games and playing
of instruments help the child acquire skill in the use of his
hands and limbs. There is no need to restrict children to
whipping tops and flying kites; in fact, kite-flying is for women (111).

Rousseau next discusses the sense of hearing; this
discussion leads him to the subject of singing. He uses
this opportunity to work in his theory about teaching music.
He then discusses the sense of taste (113-15). Always he
emphasizes the natural, the plain. The taste for meat is
unnatural as children prefer the vegetable foods, such as
fruit, milk, and pastry. He goes so far as to claim the
cruelty of a people is in direct proportion to their love of
meat, and "great criminals prepare themselves for murder
by drinking blood." Although this statement definitely dates
Rousseau, his purpose in discussing it is still valid: He
wants to warn the tutor to keep the child's primitive tastes
as long as possible by giving him only plain and simple
foods, but taking care not to make his diet too monotonous
(115-18).

After giving his views on the sense of smell, Rousseau talks of a sort of sixth sense, common sense. Rousseau claims this sense is so named "not so much because it
is common to all men, but because it results from the well-
regulated use of the other five, and teaches the nature of
things by the sum-total of their external aspects" (122).

Rousseau devotes the remainder of Book II to the
praise of childhood for having a perfection of its own. This
is the time, according to Rousseau, when the child is "keen,
eager, and full of life, free from gnawing cares and painful
forebodings, absorbed in this present state, and delighting in
a fullness of life which seems to extend beyond himself"
(123). When he described Emile at this age, Rousseau feels,
without doubt, that his pupil is superior in every way.

Book III

On Education from Twelve to Fifteen

Between twelve and fifteen, the child does not yet
have to deal with the passions which arise from puberty so
he can devote much of his time to studies which he instinc-
tively wants to learn: geography, astronomy, physics. This
is the time to introduce him to a trade in case Fortune
should ever require that he earn his own living. He still
has little knowledge, but he has the means of acquiring knowledge.

This period, the third stage of childhood, occurs before the child has reached puberty; it is a time when the

strength of the child is in excess of his wants. This is a
short and precious time. Since he cannot learn everything,
the tutor must carefully select what he learns with the selection being governed by usefulness, as well as by instinct
(128-30).[44]

      Studies based on what the child instinctively wants to
learn include geography, astronomy, and physics. The child
should have opportunities to observe the rising and setting of
the sun, in both summer and winter. Never should symbols
substitute for the thing signified (133). The child can learn
elementary physics, such as the use of magnets, when he has
an occasion to see a magnet at work and is curious about it.
He can learn the laws of statics and hydrostatics through his
own rough experiments (139). The tutor must see that some
chain of reasoning connects the experiments; thus they will
form a logical sequence in the mind and be more meaningful
and be easier to retain (140). The child should not be taught
things beyond his grasp, for of what use will those things be
to him if he does not understand them (142)? Rousseau dem-
onstrates the usefulness of learning astronomy with a vivid
example. Emile and his tutor get lost in the forest around
lunchtime; that is, Emile gets lost. The tutor intends to
let Emile find his way out by the use of the previous day's
lesson in astronomy. Emile knows how to find the north at
midday by the direction of the shadows. He knows the forest lies to the north of the town, so he has only to determine the south from the opposite direction of the shadows and
in looking to the south should discover the town. He does indeed find the town and thus proves to himself the usefulness
of astronomy (143-44).

      The child should be in competition with himself, not
with others. Most books teach things which their readers
do not really know about. Rousseau goes so far as to say:
"The child who reads ceases to think, he only reads. He is
acquiring words not knowledge" (131). Hence children should
not be given books except perhaps for one book--Robinson
Crusoe, which Rousseau describes as "the first book Emile
will read; for a long time it will form his whole library,
and it will always retain an honoured place" (147). Rousseau's praise of this book follows from his desire to make
Emile dependent upon no man and to make Emile capable of
providing his own living should such an occasion arise. It
is also in keeping with Rousseau's idea of keeping the child's
taste simple and natural, and of teaching the child respect
for all honest labor.

The child knows of the natural equality of all men;
he knows something about the concept of property. Beyond
these things, he should know nothing of government in general (152). By the same token, when once he understands the
use of money, he should not learn the abuse of money (153).

When the pupil has learned of the heavens and the
earth, it is time to turn to him as a person. Once Emile
knows what life is, he must learn how to preserve his life.
This can be done by not striving to fit him in only one station of life, but by providing him with some means in case
Fortune upsets his plans. He must then learn a trade (158).
If he never needs to work, it does not matter; as Rousseau
says: "Work for honour, not for need; stoop to the position
of a working man, to rise above your own" (159).

Since Emile will not have his choice of a trade, the
tutor will help him to choose a useful one--an "honest" trade;
and at the same time, he will learn the differences between
a liking and an aptitude (160-61). The tutor must forbid his
choosing an unhealthy trade, although a difficult or dangerous
one is not out of the question (162). The trade should be
one which requires some mental, as well as physical, effort;
since according to Rousseau: "The great secret of education
is to use exercise of mind and body as relaxation one to the
other" (165). The best trade, then, according to the tutor's
opinion, is that of carpentry. It is clean and honest work.
The tutor should be an apprentice also (163).

This apprenticeship is, in effect, Emile's debut into
the world; for it follows that it will not be long before he
discovers social inequalities. He will develop ideas in addition to his sensations; he will reason now where once he
only felt (165). He has learned to reason well, for he has
never taken any pride in merely knowing a thing, but has always
striven to avoid mistakes by considering things carefully and
attentively. Since he has had to learn for himself, he will
also use his own reason; and the tutor has achieved his goal,
that goal being, in Rousseau's words:

> not to supply him with exact knowledge, but the
> means of getting it when required, to teach him
> to value it at its true worth, and to love truth
> above all things. By this method progress is
> slow but sure, and we never need to retrace our
> steps. (170)

Book IV

On Education After Fifteen

Rousseau discusses that complex period of a child's
life during puberty. Sex education underlies the whole book.
The passions give rise to a love for humanity. Emile learns
of suffering and of men--of the former from experience; of
the latter from history and fables. He learns of women--
not from experience, which until now has been the best
teacher, but from his tutor's speeches and lessons. He
learns of God and religion, although he adopts no sect. Finally, he begins to picture his ideal mate--Sophie[45]--and to
look forward to finding her.

Rousseau believes we are born twice; first, to exist
as a human being and then, to live as a man. The years
following fifteen are years of change, both emotional and
physical. This is the time of the second birth. The child
is becoming a man, and his rising passions announce this
change (172). The origin of the passions is self-love; it is
primitive and instinctive, and as such is good, in accord
with nature. Self-preservation requires self-love. After
Emile loves himself, he will love others around him. At
this time selfishness may spring up. Although self-love is
content to satisfy one's needs, selfishness is always making
comparisons and is never satisfied. Self-love is then the
source of the tender gentle passions; whereas selfishness is
the source for the hateful, angry passions (173-75).

The child of fifteen has to learn to cope with both
kinds of passions. It may be time for the tutor to speak to
his pupil on the subject of sex education. If there is any
way to delay this discussion without unduly arousing curiosity
or suspicion, then delay. If the tutor cannot put the subject
off, he should answer in a straight forward plain manner,
without mystery, confusion, or smiling, or even hesitating.
This manner is more likely to stop curiosity than to encourage it. Naturally, the tutor should tell the truth, although
he may tell it in such a way as to discourage more questions
(177). For example, Rousseau praises the mother who in
answer to the child's question, "Where do little children come
from?" answered: "Women pass them with pains that sometimes cost their life." Rousseau claims that this answer
will lead the child to think of the results of childbirth, not
the causes (179).

Rousseau sums up human wisdom with regard to the
passions as: "First, to be conscious of the true relations
of man both in the species and the individual; second, to
control all the affections in accordance with these relations"
(180).

Before the youth is capable of love of the opposite
sex, he is capable of friendship. The tutor should take advantage of this time to see that the child learns of true humanity (181). Since man's weakness makes him sociable,
it is the common misery of mankind which inclines one
toward humanity. A hermit should be a truly happy man,
for he is strong enough to be self-sufficient. But if one has
need of nothing, how can he love anything? A hermit must
then be wretched and alone (182). Man is drawn toward his
fellow-creatures; and, in fact, there are several maxims
which apply to man's relationship with other men. The first,
according to Rousseau, is: "It is not in human nature to
put ourselves in the place of those who are happier than ourselves, but only in the place of those who can claim our pity" (184). The second is: "We never pity another's woes
unless we know we may suffer in like manner ourselves"
(185). Thus the tutor must teach his pupil that he stands on
the edge of an abyss from which Fortune may at any time
fling him downward (185). For the pupil to understand fully,
Rousseau says the tutor should

> let him see and feel the calamities which overtake
> men; surprise and startle his imagination with the
> perils which lurk continually about a man's path;
> let him see the pitfalls all about him, and when he
> hears you speak of them, let him cling more close-
> ly to you for fear lest he should fall. (186)

And the third maxim is stated as: "The pity we feel for
others is proportionate, not to the amount of evil, but to the
feelings we attribute to the sufferers" (186). This maxim
would explain to a certain extent cruelty to animals.

Emile must learn to love all men (187); [46] then he
will be able to share the suffering of another but at the same
time, he shares it of his own free will so he finds pleasure
in it and does not become melancholy (190-91). However,
he must not see too much pain or suffering, or his heart
may grow hardened to it as priests and doctors grow
hardened. Instead, a selected example at just the right
moment may fill his heart and cause him to think for several

weeks thereafter (192).

    In addition to learning of humanity, the youth should
be prevented, if possible, from growing up all at once (193).
Remove the youth from the city (192) and take advantage of
his youthful enthusiasm to acquire a hold on his heart (194).
Emile must learn about society and about men and about the
mask that society forces men to wear (197-98). But at this
time, the tutor should reverse his former maxim of experience as the best teacher. Now it is better to give him lessons rather than let him experience before he is fully ready
(199).

    To know men, Emile can learn the action of men from
history books, but history in general is lacking because it
does not give a true picture. The historian embellishes his
accounts with fictitious details or even with his own opinions.
He also oversimplifies and dwells on evil deeds, not good
ones; he gives accounts of nations as they go to war and are
in a state of decline. If the nation is growing and peaceful,
the historian does not concern himself with these facts (200-
201). The modern historian is worse than the ancient one
when it comes to coloring portraits of people. In fact, the
historian does not picture the private lives of people; hence
biography is better for learning about men than history is
(202).

    For the proper study of men, Emile will need, ac-
cording to Rousseau: "a great wish to know men, great im-
partiality of judgment, a heart sufficiently sensitive to understand every human passion, and calm enough to be free from
passion" (206). The tutor must beware that his student does
not get too high an opinion of himself when he realizes he is
wiser and happier than most. Man can be cured of any fault
except vanity (207). At this delicate time, the tutor must
not pretend to be too wise; he must warn his pupil of faults
and dangers beforehand, but never never say, "I told you so"
(209).

    At this time of faults, fables can serve a constructive
end. The writer of fables is foolish to put a moral at the
end, for if the moral is not clear from the tale itself, a
few lines at the end will not help; in fact, they will only de-
prive the student of his pleasure of figuring out the moral
for himself. Never should the tutor simply follow the order
of fables as they appear in a book; he should correlate them
with the requirements of the child and with his particular

situation (210-11).

   The youth should learn to be good by doing good. He
should help those in need not merely with his money, but
with his person and his time (212). Emile does not like
fighting among either men or animals. He will never set
two animals fighting. He will try to reconcile his comrades
who fight; he should try to ascertain the cause of any suffering and alleviate it (213).

   By now Emile has learned to think, but he hardly
knows what a philosopher or God is (217). Rousseau speci-
fies: "At fifteen he will not even know that he has a soul,
at eighteen even he may not be ready to learn about it"
(220). Emile has not been taught religion for a good reason.
As a child, he could not grasp the complex and confusing
ideas of creation, destruction, eternity, almighty power, and
other characteristics of God. Once he is taught what he
does not understand, he can be made to say anything (218-
19). Also, the faith of children and the faith of some adults
depends solely on geography--those born near Rome are of
one religion; those near Mecca of another (220). If once a
child gets an incorrect idea of God in his head, he will likely retain that idea all of his life; and thus as an adult, he
will not understand any more than he did as a child (222).

   Rousseau prefers not to attach Emile to any particular sect. He justifies this choice by a lengthy digression
entitled "The Creed of a Savoyard Priest" (228-78). This
digression is complex, beginning with the first cause and including a discussion of God, human will, judgment, evil, immortality, justice, suffering, goodness, prayer, the Scrip-
tures, a dialogue between Reason and Inspiration, religions
other than Catholicism, and other subjects. Rousseau clearly believes in God; his religion is more Deism than anything else; he believes what he himself can know by turning
inward. Yet his approach is often emotional in spite of the
fact that he thinks he is being strictly rational. He says,
for example, that while he does not know if body and soul
both die together, there is no reason to assume that the soul
might not live on. He accepts this assumption because it is
not unreasonable and it is consoling (246). He rejects divine
revelation and miracles; he closes the Bible and opens the
book of nature, written in a language all men can understand
(270). In regard to other religions, he believes God rejects
no homage that is sincere (272).

After Emile is introduced to religion, he is complete
in every way save one: his desire for a mate or marriage.
To prevent an unfortunate incident, he could marry very
young; but this method is not best. It is better to treat him
as a friend and a man; and he will open his heart to his
faithful tutor. The tutor should never preach to him or
scold him, or he will cease to tell what is in his heart. To
protect him from women unworthy of him, his tutor should
provide him with a new and pleasant occupation which will
occupy both his time and his mind--hunting. Although Rousseau is not in favor of this cruel sport usually, he does feel
that it can serve the purpose of delaying a more dangerous
passion for a while (285).

When Emile has come to rely upon his tutor and desires to please him, then it is time for the tutor to describe
marriage to Emile in glowing terms and to disparage de-
bauchery in vivid terms (288-89). Emile at twenty is ready
to enter society. His tutor has properly prepared him and
in the case of the opposite sex, properly warned him. He
will be polite and well-liked in no time, although no one will
call him a wit, a great talker, or a great charmer (292,
301, 304). It is possible to delay one's entry into society
too long, which will make for awkwardness and constraint
(293). It is time when he enters society to describe his perfect mate to him so he will have a clear idea about the kind
of person he will someday marry; the tutor names her Sophie
(294).

The tutor must watch over Emile; no one becomes
corrupt at once nor skilled in the art of deception without
practice (298). There is no need to worry about what others
may encourage or mock him to do, for Emile has learned
not to care about the criticisms of others (296).

Rousseau next discusses taste as the subject Emile
should now take up. Taste, according to his definition, is
"merely the power of judging what is pleasing or displeasing
to most people. " It involves things which are indifferent to
us, not those related to our needs (305). All true models
of taste can be found in nature; thus true taste is simple,
not lavish; good taste implies good morals. Women are to
be judges of good taste in bodily matters, but men are the
best judges of matters of morality and understanding. Rousseau continues:

but since [women] have set themselves up as

judges of literature, since they have begun to
criticize books and to make them might and main,
they are altogether astray. Authors who take the
advice of blue-stockings will always be ill-advised;
gallants who consult them about their clothes will
always be absurdly dressed. (306)

After criticizing the blue-stockings, Rousseau criti-
cizes Paris as the center of bad taste, yet the place where
good taste is cultivated (307). As for taste in books, Emile
will prefer the ancients over the moderns because the former
were closer to nature and their genius more distinct. Emile
will go to the theater to study taste, not morals. The stage
is not the place for truth; its purpose is to flatter and a-
muse (309). A study of theater leads to a study of poetry:
both have the same purpose. Poetry will provide unlimited
amusement and be a delight to Emile.

The last lesson of Book IV is a varied one. It is a
detailed description of what the tutor would do and how he
would live if he were rich. It is simply a restatement of
many ideas presented earlier: live close to nature; eat
simple foods; keep only a few servants; live in a simple
house, not a palace; do not collect anything like books, for
collections can never be complete; do not gamble; do not try
to buy friends or a mistress; do not spend money in pursuit
of empty dreams; take each day as it comes; be one's own
servant in order to be one's own master; do not have any
monopolies; leave Paris, and begin to search for Sophie.

Book V

On Education of Girls and Final Steps to Manhood

Rousseau begins his last book by stating that he will
not, like Locke, leave his young gentleman about to marry.
Instead he tells of Sophie, her education, her preparation for
marriage with Emile. He takes Emile and Sophie through a
tender courtship and separation of two years during which
Emile learns of travel and government, of his duties as a
citizen. Finally the two marry; and upon learning of an ap-
proaching birth, Emile desires to teach the child himself.
After all, the father is the best teacher. The book closes
with Emile telling his tutor to continue his work; he will always need him. [47]

In discussing Sophie's education, Rousseau claims that

the education of a woman should be suited to her role in life.
He points out that women are much like men except in regard
to sex, where each is the complement of the other (321).   A
woman should be weak and passive while her husband should
be strong and active.   Her function is to please men; her
strength lies in her charm (322).   She should, however, receive care during the periods when she is not strong: during pregnancy and the period following.   She has charge of
the child's education; she alone can make the father feel the
joys of fatherhood (324).   She must take care not only to be
faithful, but also to maintain a good reputation.   She should
have about four children; for two will probably die before
adulthood, and the other two are necessary to replace their
parents (325).

        Rousseau believes it good that there are no colleges
for girls, for colleges for boys do not do a good job with
boys.   Girls are to learn enough to be a helpmate and companion to their husbands (327).   Their duties in life are to
please men and care for them at every age (328).   They are
to have physical training, not for the purpose of developing
strength, but for the purpose of becoming graceful.   They
are to wear loose garments just as boys should.   Corsets
are in poor taste; they distort the natural figure (330).

        Little girls are to have dolls to play with.   As they
learn to care for their dolls, so they are preparing themselves for motherhood.   Their desire to dress their dolls in
pretty clothes can motivate them to learn sewing.   They may
then learn embroidery, lacemaking, drawing; but they usually
do not like to read or write (331).

        Young girls should be subjected to more authority than
boys because they are more precocious and need to learn to
be docile; however, they should not have to do things for
which they see no reason (331).

        Self-control is all-important for girls.   Idleness and
insubordination are bad faults which they must not develop.
Girls tend to carry things to extremes; this tendency must
be checked, for it is the source of caprice and fickleness.
They may run, and jump, and laugh, and be happy so long
as they are somewhat restrained (333).

        Girls and women desire fine clothes; they should learn
that these things are necessary only to hide their flaws, so
the more recourse they have to them, the more defects they

must have. There is no need to change styles all the time;
if a style suits a young lady, she should keep it. There is
no reason to spend hours at her toilet, although she should
dress carefully (335-36).

Singing and dancing are innocent pleasures of youth
and should be permitted (337). A young girl should develop
the art of speaking. Women talk more than men; but this
fact is to their credit, for they say what will please; but
men say what they know (339).

Instead of the rule of usefulness that boys have, girls
should always ask, "What effect will that have?" They should
also have the rule never to tell a lie. They need not, however, be deprived of religion, like boys, until the age of
reason. As they are unlikely ever to be able to grasp religion, it does not hurt to expose them to it at an early age.
Daughters should follow their mothers' religion; wives their
husbands'. Unfortunately, there is no truly adequate cate-
chism for children (341). The mother should take care to
answer the child's questions and teach her the fundamentals,
such as: There is a God; we are His children; we should
love Him and one another; we should be just and keep our
word. We should expect judgment in the life to come.
Daughters do not need to be theologians; they need to learn
only those doctrines which are conducive to goodness (344).

Girls should be taught to reconcile the law of public
opinion with that of individual conscience. The judge between these two is reason (345). In addition to reason, hon-
or of position as a woman, no matter what station in life,
is important. Women are to be what nature made them to
be. Their studies, therefore, should be practical. They
need no knowledge of philosophy or science (349). They are
not the great thinkers; men have genius; women have wit.
Women observe; whereas men reason (350).

It is a mother's job to be her daughter's companion,
to expose her daughter to balls and theaters so she will
learn the proper attitude toward them. A mother should not
bring her daughter to Paris, however, just for this purpose.
She should explain her daughter's duties to her, but in a
pleasant way so as not to make her dislike them (350-53).
The more important and difficult duties require more care in
explaining the reasons for them. A mother who says, "Be
good," will never succeed like a mother who shows her
daughter that it is in her daughter's best interest to be good.

At this time a mother should help her daughter form a picture of a good husband. This picture is to protect her when she meets other men who are not worthy (355).

Rousseau turns to Sophie now and describes her at length; in all ways she fits the description of a girl reared according to Rousseau's principles for educating girls. She is well-born and has a good disposition. She is not beautiful, but she arouses interest; knowing how to dress, she always appears simple, yet elegant (357). She is skilled in those feminine occupations of needlework, lacemaking, housekeeping, cooking, cleaning, keeping household accounts. Temperate in both habit and virtue, she eats sparingly, enjoying sweets, milk, and pastry, but little meat (357-58).

To make Sophie appear to be human, Rousseau adds the fault of her having whims. Another so-called fault, that of not always being good humored, results from her sensitive nature.

Sophie does not gossip; she has little knowledge of society or of that vain habit of wearing high heels. She is indignant at overly sentimental speeches made for her amusement (360-61). In fact, Sophie is so trustworthy and reliable that her parents will permit her to choose her own husband. She should marry for love, not wealth or position. Her parents married for love and have always been very happy (363-64).

Sophie leaves the country and stays with her aunt for a while in the city in hope of finding a husband. No one pleases her, and she returns home where she is despondent. Upon questioning her, her mother learns that Sophie is in love with Telemachus, the hero of Fénelon's prose epic, The Adventures of Telemachus. No one appears as noble to her as her ideal, fictional hero; that is, no one until she meets Emile (365-68). Emile's tutor contrives their meeting, and it is a case of love at first sight. Emile and his tutor have been traveling, but now they settle in a village several miles from Sophie's house so that their courtship can begin (381).

The courtship is a happy time; the two come to know each other quite well, although they do not see each other every day. When they are not together, they spend their days doing good deeds. Finally Sophie accepts Emile's offer, but the tutor tells Emile he should learn of his duty as a citizen in order to protect Sophie and give her a good life.

Also he should know her longer; they should grow up more--
she is not yet eighteen and he is only twenty-two. He should
see if either his love or her love fades through separation.
These things should be done before marriage (411-12).

Emile agrees to a separation of two years during
which time he travels with his tutor. Rousseau then inserts
his digression, "Of Travel" (414ff.). It is from traveling in
the proper manner that Emile will learn of men and of nations. He will learn of government and of citizenship. He
will then ideally be in a position to know where and in what
manner he wants to live for the rest of his life with his
bride (419).

According to Rousseau, the purpose of travel is to
learn of men and nations, not to dig in libraries and muse-
ums to learn of centuries ago. When one has seen a dozen
Frenchmen, he has seen them all (415). Only those strong
enough to see error and vice should undertake travel (418).
A country's capital is no place to learn of the people of that
country. The remote provinces are the places to go to learn
what a people is truly like and how successful their government is (432-33); travel in these remote regions will also
protect the youth from the vice of the cities (434).

In traveling, Emile will learn of government by study-
ing, as Rousseau puts it, "the nature of government in general, then the different forms of government, and lastly the
particular government under which he was born, to know if
it suits him to live under it" (419). Rousseau takes this opportunity to expound briefly on his theory of government
which he develops in his <u>Treatise on the Social Contract</u>, a
work which he claims in a footnote to have long since aban-
doned (426). (He must have taken it up again, for it was
published later in the same year that <u>Emile</u> was.)

At the end of his travels and his study of government,
Emile concludes that he will not be dependent upon his inheritance; rich or poor, he will be free. He says:

> What matters my place in the world? What mat-
> ters it where I am? Wherever there are men, I
> am among my brethren; wherever there are none,
> I am in my own home. So long as I may be in-
> dependent and rich, and have wherewithal to live,
> and I shall live. If my wealth makes a slave of
> me, I shall find it easy to renounce it. I have

hands to work, and I shall get a living. . . . Whensoever death comes I defy it; it shall never find me making preparation for life; it shall never prevent me having lived. (436)

The tutor, pleased with Emile's speech, goes on to say: "Liberty is not to be found in any form of government; she is in the heart of the free man, he bears her with him everywhere" (437).

Emile and Sophie marry. The tutor offers advice on the state of marriage also: each should give to the other through love and his own wish to please, not through obligation or duty. The book closes with Emile informing his tutor that a child is on the way and giving his thanks to his tutor. He will teach his own child; but at the same time, he claims he will need his tutor now, in taking up the duties of manhood, more than ever before. (The irony of this dependence has been pointed out earlier.)

Notes

1. For additional information on editions and publication in the British Isles, see J. H. Warner, "Emile in Eighteenth-Century England," PMLA, LIX (1944), 774.

2. The reasons for the popularity of these works among children are discussed in Paul Hazard, Books, Children, and Men, trans. Marguerite Mitchell (Boston: The Horn Book, Inc., 1944), p. 47-68.

3. Montrose J. Moses, Children's Books and Reading (New York: Mitchell Kennerley, 1907), p. 63.

4. F. J. Harvey Darton, Children's Books in England: Five Centuries of Social Life (Cambridge at the University Press, 1932), p. 141.

5. May H. Arbuthnot, Children and Books (rev. ed.; Chicago Scott, Foresman and Co., 1957), p. 47.

6. Mary F. Thwaite, From Primer to Pleasure: An Introduction to the History of Children's Books in England, from the Invention of Printing to 1900, with a Chapter on Some Developments Abroad (London: Library Association, 1963), p. 64.

7. Ibid., p. 211.

8. Cornelia Lynde Meigs, "Roots in the Past up to 1840,"
    A Critical History of Children's Literature: A Sur-
    vey of Children's Books in English from Earliest
    Times to the Present, Prepared in 4 pts., ed.
    Cornelia L. Meigs (New York: Macmillan, 1953,
    p. 94.

9. Elva Sophronia Smith, The History of Children's Litera-
    ture: A Syllabus with Selected Bibliographies (Chi-
    cago: American Library Association, 1937), p. 71.

10. Florence Valentine Barry, A Century of Children's
    Books (New York: George H. Doran Co., 1923),
    p. 86.

11. Ibid., p. 122.

12. Meigs, p. 97.

13. Bess Porter Adams, About Books and Children: His-
    torical Survey of Children's Literature (New York:
    Henry Holt and Co., Inc., 1953), p. 50.

14. Moses, p. 63.

15. R. H. Eliassen, "Rousseau Under the Searchlights of
    Modern Education," American Book Collector, XII
    (Summer, 1962), 13-14.   Eliassen's article was
    written in recognition of the 200th birthday of the
    publication of Emile. The author gives a good sum-
    mary of the negative points in Rousseau's theory;
    that is, those which are incorrect and/or outdated;
    but he writes, of course, of Rousseau's contribu-
    tions to educational theory, not to children's litera-
    ture.

16. This list has been compiled after consulting the follow-
    ing sources as to who the primary writers were:
    Adams, Barry, Darton, Meigs, Moses, Muir, Os-
    borne, Shaw, Smith, Thwaite, and others. It is
    noted that many books of poetry and songs for chil-
    dren, either read by them or to them, must be
    omitted. Yet at least this brief mention of Gold-
    smith, Cowper, Gray, Blake, the Taylors, and Lucy
    Aikin will show that the authors of children's books

were branching out into other genres. Periodicals
for children also made an appearance in the late
eighteenth century. A brief summary of them is
given in M. F. Thwaite, p. 221-23.

17. The British Museum Catalogue was used to distinguish
between the Kilner sisters' works. The only known
dates are roughly 1783-1790, with the exception of
Jemima Placid, whose date is known to be 1788.

18. André Boutet de Monvel, "Introduction," to Emile,
trans. Barbara Foxley (London: Dent, 1911), p. vi.
For a complete chronological list of Rousseau's
writings on education, see Minor Educational Writings, trans. William Boyd (New York: Columbia
University, 1962), p. 104-105.

19. Leonora Blanche Lang, Men, Women and Minxes (London: Longman's, 1913), p. 169.

20. Minor Educational Writings, Intro., William Boyd, p. 6.

21. Adams, p. 43-44, credits these points to Locke, but
they would also apply to Rousseau.

22. James Phinney Munroe, The Educational Ideal: An
Outline of Its Growth in Modern Times (Boston:
D. C. Heath and Co., 1909), p. 154.

23. F[rederick] C[harles] Green, Jean-Jacques Rousseau:
A Critical Study of His Life and Writings (Cambridge:
Cambridge University Press, 1955), p. 263.

24. Gabriel Compayré, Jean Jacques Rousseau and Education from Nature, trans. R. P. Jago (New York:
Thomas Y. Crowell Co., 1907), p. 1.

25. James H. Warner, "The Basis of J. -J. Rousseau's
Contemporaneous Reputation in England," MLN, LV
(1940), 280.

26. Pages in parentheses in body of text refer to Foxley's
translation.

27. Lang, p. 173, among others, points out this contradiction.

28. Barry, p. 90.

29. R. L. Archer (ed.), Jean Jacques Rousseau: His Educational Theories Selected from Emile, Julie and Other Writings (Woodbury, N. Y.: Barron's Educational Series, Inc., 1964), p. 14. Others have sought to show that Rousseau's works are not contradictory. For a good survey on the lack of contradiction, see Ernst Cassirer, The Question of Jean-Jacques Rousseau, trans. and ed. Peter J. Gay (New York: Columbia University Press, 1954).

30. Minor Educational Writings, p. 2.

31. Compayré, p. 100-101.

32. Henri Roddier, J. -J. Rousseau en Angleterre au XVIIIe siècle: L'oeuvre et l'homme (Paris: Boivin, 1950), p. 177.

33. The Educational Ideal, p. 172.

34. John Morley, Rousseau (2 vols.; London: Macmillan, 1915), II, 249-50.

35. PMLA, LIX, 774n.

36. Ibid., p. 776.

37. Ibid., p. 781-90. Only the names have been listed here; the reader should see these pages and their footnotes for what was said and where it was said.

38. Ibid., p. 791.

39. These sentiments at first seem ironic in light of the fact that the author gave his five children away to an orphans' home, but numerous critics point out that Rousseau always regretted that action and even wrote Emile for all children as partial restitution to the children he gave up.

40. This is one of his points which found the least acceptance and is today still rejected.

41. The idea is not original, for some eleven years earlier, John Marchant in the "Preface" to Puerilia (London:

Printed for the author, 1751), p. vi. , mentions it.

42. It is interesting that Rousseau does not mention animals, only human beings--for cruelty to animals is
one of the major themes of children's literature of
the period.

43. Rousseau does not seem to object to this kind of deceit, nor does he seem to realize that striving for
the plain dark frame is merely an inversion of values with a reward being the object in both cases.

44. Green, p. 233, has pointed out that Rousseau's belief
in the development of certain faculties of the mind
at certain periods of life--sensibility, intelligence,
will--which give rise to a corresponding order of
psychic facts was traditional psychology for the period, Aristotle's theory as modified by Descartes.

45. In Foxley's translation the name is spelled Sophy, but
this is the only work which I have seen that uses
this spelling; consequently, I will follow the majority.

46. A few pages later, Rousseau says Emile should respect
the individual, but despise the multitude (198).

47. This need appears to be a contradiction to Emile's independence.

Chapter II

Anna Laetitia Barbauld and John Aikin

The main purpose of children's stories of the late
eighteenth century was to teach. Every writer of children's
books of the period broke two of Rousseau's cardinal rules:
(1) they wrote for an audience which Rousseau said was too
young to be reading; and (2) they were, in effect, telling
children their lessons rather than having the children experience them for themselves. In regard to the first point, all
the books included in this study were written for children under fifteen, the age at which Emile is permitted to read.
Perhaps Rousseau's delayed reading program for Emile was
a result of a lack of suitable material for children to read.
In regard to the second point, perhaps Rousseau would have
permitted vicarious learning experiences, but again there
were no suitable books. It is, of course, useless to specu-
late on what Rousseau might have changed had there been
books to fill the need.

Anna Laetitia Barbauld was one of the first to recognize this need. Her works in turn served as a model for
other works; for example, Lessons for Children was a model
for Sarah Trimmer's Easy Introduction to the Knowledge of
Nature, and Thomas Day also read it with interest before he
began his writings for children. Richard Edgeworth began
Harry and Lucy with the idea of continuing Mrs. Barbauld's
good work.

Mrs. Barbauld states her ideas about education in the
essay, "On Education," which she wrote for a wealthy gentleman and father who had inquired about her views on the
subject. Miss Lucy Aikin, her niece, dates this essay
"amongst her later pieces."[1] The date is less important,
however, than her recognition of a flaw in Rousseau's plan,
a flaw which she calls an Achilles heel; the flaw is that "im-
perious circumstances forbid . . . the practice of [his
plan]."[2]

It is significant that if the piece is dated late in her

career, then it comes after her experience of teaching
Charles, her brother's son, whom she adopted at less than
two years of age. It was for Charles that she wrote Lessons
for Children. The essay also comes after her eleven years
of experience as a teacher in her husband's boarding school
for boys in the village of Palgrave in Suffolk.[3] During this
period from 1775-1786, she wrote Hymns in Prose for Children, especially for several pupils at the school whom she
wished to introduce to literature and to religion. Thus, Mrs.
Barbauld had considerable practical experience in education.

This first female writer of children's books in England had much more education and book learning than she
would advocate for most young ladies. She says, for example: "I am full well convinced that to have a too great fondness for books is little favourable to the happiness of a woman, especially one not in affluent circumstances. My situation has been peculiar, and would be no rule for others."[4]

When encouraged by such people as Mrs. Montague
to begin a school for young ladies shortly before she and her
husband began the boys' school, Mrs. Barbauld wrote some
comments on the education of girls, ideas which appear to
coincide beautifully with Rousseau's:

> But young ladies, who ought only to have such a
> general tincture of knowledge as to make them
> agreeable companions to a man of sense, and to
> enable them to find rational entertainment for a
> solitary hour, should gain these accomplishments
> in a more quiet and unobserved manner. . . .[5]

Mrs. Barbauld agrees further with Rousseau in her
suggestion that geography, language, and grammar are best
for ages nine through thirteen or fourteen. By fifteen, it is
too late to begin to learn because the passions come into the
picture. If a girl of fifteen has the foundation laid for her
studies, she can carry on without a master, or in Mrs. Barbauld's words, "with such a one only as Rousseau gives his
Sophie." She further states that the girl's mother is her
best tutor in this period when she needs to learn grace and
polish in society, as well as domestic duties and the proper
behavior toward the opposite sex.[6]

In her ideas about the education of girls, it is clear
that Rousseau had a definite impact upon Mrs. Barbauld.
But the children's books which Mrs. Barbauld wrote were,

as stated earlier, written for boys. Mrs. Barbauld's views
on female education have been interjected here to prove that
she knew Rousseau's <u>Emile</u> well: she also knew it before the
opening of the Palgrave school in 1775 and hence before writing both <u>Lessons for Children</u> (1780) and <u>Hymns in Prose for
Children</u> (1781). This conclusion would agree with that of
one critic who states that Mrs. Barbauld's husband was of
"French connections" and thus she "took note of Rousseau
early."[7]

Lessons for Children

        Mrs. Barbauld states the purpose of her first book
for children in the "Preface." She wrote <u>Lessons for Chil-
dren</u>, the first of four parts, for children from two to four
years old. Mrs. Barbauld recognized what the capacity of a
child that age was, and furthermore she recognized what all
publishers of children's books today know: the importance
of easily readable type, as well as the importance of ar-
rangement and spacing on a page. She claims her "task is
humble, but not mean; for to lay the first stone of a noble
building, and to plant the first idea in a human mind, can be
no dishonour to any hand."[8]

        The purpose then was to teach the child to read and
at the same time to teach him useful information, as, for example, about weather or about food--things the child comes
in contact with in everyday life. The other three parts of
the work--<u>Lessons for Children, of Four Years Old, from
Four to Five Years Old</u>, and <u>from Five to Six Years Old</u>--
teach more difficult, yet still useful, information, and not by
way of constant repetition as many primary readers of this
century do. Rousseau could not have objected to the lessons
taught in these books; he might, however, have objected to
the fact that most tutors could not set up a situation where
the child could discover gold, silver, tin, steel and the other
metals which Mrs. Barbauld describes. Mrs. Barbauld's so-
lution, while less vivid than Rousseau's, is the more practical. Let the child discover through books what he does not
discover through actual experience. Charles Lamb was to
criticize Mrs. Barbauld for cramming children full of natural
history while doing nothing to further their creative abilities;[9]
and he also condemned both her and Mrs. Trimmer in a letter to Coleridge in 1802 for leading juvenile literature
astray.[10]

The first part of Lessons for Children, from Two to Four Years Old is of necessity without plot and character development. It is a series of lessons with little relation to one another. There is much admonition and few examples of teaching by experience. The following excerpt shows the relationship, such as it is, between the ideas:

> The sun shines. Open your eyes,
> little boy. Get up.
> Maid, come and dress Charles.
> Go down stairs. Get your breakfast.
> Boil some milk for a poor little hungry boy.
> Do not spill the milk.
> Hold the spoon in the other hand.
> Do not throw your bread upon the ground.
> Bread is to eat, you must not throw it away.
> Corn makes bread.
> Corn grows in the fields.
> Grass grows in the fields.
> Cows eat grass, and sheep eat grass,
> and horses eat grass.
> Little boys do not eat grass: no,
> they eat bread and milk.[11]

The vocabulary is necessarily limited; the brief consideration of many subjects and the lack of concentration on any one subject are more likely to hold the interest of the very young child.

The subjects treated which show the influence of Rousseau are the knowledge of nature (33), the knowledge and exercise involved in helping bring in the wood and sweep the hearth (27), the idea that a young child should be taught to swim (15), the beginning of the concept of generosity in the child's giving some money to a poor little boy at the door (101). Rousseau, of course, did not advocate teaching religion to the young child. It is interesting to note that this work is written for a child about the same age as the children for whom Hymns in Prose was written and that both cover many of the same subjects, as the seasons, animals, and insects; but here there is no mention of religion.

There are differences from Rousseau's practices. Young Charles is able to write upon his slate (29) at a much younger age than Emile could; Charles cannot have meat for dinner because he has a cough (44)--Rousseau would forbid meat at all times; Charles' parent or tutor can say to him

at times, "Go away now, I am busy" (45). Emile's tutor
could never utter these words.

In Lessons for Children of Four Years Old, Part I,
the child, after learning the days of the week (5), learns
about every month in the year with the high lights of each
month pointed out to him. For example, January is cold;
things freeze; it is the time for skating (9-10). June is the
time when men and children are working in the hayfields (21).
It is the time for gathering currants and strawberries (23).
By November the weather is cold; but clear. The leaves
and the flowers are gone, but there are nuts now to be
cracked (38).

Again there is little plot or character development.
The lessons, based mainly on animals, come one right after
the other. Charles learns about the feet of animals (43-44),
wings of birds (45), where animals live (53-54), noises animals make (54-56), feeding birds in winter (71).

The feeding of the birds brings up one of the two
short stories included at the end. The first story (73-77) is
typical of many others during this period, the authors of
which resort to very cruel endings to prove their point. A
naughty boy will not feed a starving and freezing robin; in
fact, he even pulls the poor bird's tail! It dies. Shortly
after that, the boy's parents leave him because he is cruel,
and he is forced to beg for food. He goes into a forest,
sits down and cries, and is never heard of again; it is believed that bears ate him. This nightmare-inspiring story
seems a cruel way to instill kindness in a child. Yet Rousseau would have a child get sick in a draft to see the results of his having broken a window.

Part I closes with a story which concludes with a
moral. Rousseau, of course, did not believe in stating the
moral, but in letting the child figure it out for himself.

Part II opens by comparing Charles with cats and dogs;
the latter cannot read or talk (3-6). Part II has no development of plot or character. The subjects are again very
loosely tied together; for example, since Charles has the ability to read and talk he should learn his lessons (7). What
are they but the position of the sun at rising, at noon, and
at sunset (7-8), facts which Emile learned in a more vivid
manner, but at a much later age.

The subjects treated again are everyday ones.
Charles sees a caterpillar change into a butterfly (32-36); he
learns about the metals and stones found in the ground--gold,
silver, copper, brass, iron, steel, lead, tin, quicksilver,
marble, stones and flint and gravel, chalk and fuller's earth,
coal (53-71). He learns of the precious stones--the diamond,
ruby, emerald, topaz, sapphire, amethyst, garnet, beryl
(71-73). Mrs. Barbauld tells him about the parts of trees
and flowers and the names of the male and the female and
the young for many different animals, as the horse, lion,
tiger, bull (75-84). Rousseau would not oppose any of this
knowledge, but he could not teach much of it to Emile; for
there might not be an emerald or some chalk available to
have Emile accidentally stumble across; to merely tell Emile
about these things would not suit Rousseau's purpose.

Again there are two stories with a little plot, but
still no character development. One is the story (40-52) of
a lamb who disobeys and stays outside the fold one night.
Her punishment is drastic. A wolf and two cubs eat her.
There is no explicit statement of a moral. The other story
(87-95) does not fit Rousseau's idea of punishment suited to
the crime. A little boy is a coward; he is afraid of dogs
and goats. A dog comes to play with him; in his fear the
boy falls into a ditch from which he cannot escape. The dog
runs to the boy's house and brings his family to the ditch.
The boy is saved. Again there is no explicit statement of
moral; but this boy is very lucky that he does not receive
punishment in a manner befitting a coward.

Lessons for Children from Four to Five Years Old is
obviously written for an older child than the previous lessons
were. It consists of a fable, a short story about three
cakes,[12] and an account of a trip to France, along with a
few isolated bits of information. The fable is that of Chanticleer and Reynard (4-12). Mrs. Barbauld did not oppose
fables for children, or fairy tales for that matter, as the
discussion of Evenings at Home shows. The short story
(13-29) compares three boys and their actions when each receives a cake. Harry eats it all himself and is sick; Peter
Careful eats only a little each day, but soon it grows dry and
moldy and the mice get it. Billy shares his cake, putting
one piece aside for the next day. A blind old fiddler and his
little dog come up and play a tune for the boys. As he plays,
tears run down the fiddler's cheeks. He cries because of
hunger; Billy gives him that leftover piece of cake. This is
a vivid example of the true generosity which Rousseau en-

couraged Emile to develop.

The trip to France gives its author a chance to take
her pupil to see things which he never had occasion to see
before. For example, the teacher and pupil pass a water
wheel (40) and thus an occasion arises to learn about its op-
eration, in the manner of Rousseau's tutor. The child learns
how important it is to be able to swim (41). The child and
his tutor discover a bridge, some different trees, some
squirrels and flying squirrels and finally the sea (46-51).
The child learns there is no bridge large enough to span the
sea, so boats are used. He learns the parts of the boat
(53-54). Then they arrive in France. Here everyone speaks
French, which the little boy cannot understand. He resolves
to leave France and not come back until his papa has taught
him French (71-76). This is an excellent example of a
child's learning from practical experience, and it emphasizes
the desire to learn on the child's part which Rousseau felt
was essential. What could be a better way of inspiring the
child to learn French?

The isolated bits of information are like most of Mrs.
Barbauld's tidbits--related to nature. There is a discussion
of the number of legs on various animals (73-74), the cat's
newborn kittens (81-83), a brood of chickens (85), a description of a swan, told from the swan's point of view (90-95),
the story of the sun, told from his point of view (96-104),
and finally the moon puts in a few words (105-107). Specu-
lating is dangerous, and yet it seems probable that Rousseau
would not have objected to any of this information, but he
would have objected to those parts delivered in first person.
Naturally, the swan, the sun, and the moon do not really
talk. Their talking borders on the unrealistic, that area
where the fairy tale exists.

As Lessons for Children, from Five to Six Years
Old[13] appears to rehash much material from Part II of Four
Years Old and from Five to Six Years Old, it will be omitted
from this discussion.

In Lessons for Children, then, Mrs. Barbauld used example, fable, admonition, stated moral, and on at least one occasion, she did not use Rousseau's idea of punishment fitting
the crime. On the other hand, Harry's getting sick from
eating too much cake is a perfect punishment for his crime.
She disregarded Rousseau at will, but echoed his ideas
throughout in learning from experience, in giving the child

the desire to learn, in teaching him the concept of generosity, in teaching the child kindness to animals; and even in
emphasizing the fact that he should learn to swim. Mrs.
Barbauld's second work, Hymns in Prose shows perhaps less
influence by Rousseau than the Lessons do because of the religious nature of the Hymns.

Hymns in Prose for Children

The purpose of Hymns in Prose is, in the words of
Mrs. Barbauld's "Preface":

> to impress devotional feelings as early as possible
> on the infant mind . . . to impress them by con-
> necting religion with a variety of sensible objects;
> with all that he sees, all he hears, all that affects
> his young mind with wonder or delight; and thus by
> deep, strong and permanent associations to lay the
> best foundation for practical devotion in future
> life. [14]

This view of religious devotion impressed upon the
young mind is in direct opposition to Rousseau's shielding
Emile from religion in his early years.

It is possible, however, that Mrs. Barbauld felt Rousseau's influence in another way. The everyday objects that
she points out to Charles are, in general, those found in na-
ture--the animals, the fields, the flowers. She allows, then,
the child to discover nature as Rousseau wanted him to, but
she goes a step further. She emphasizes the relationship between nature and God. [15]

The Hymns were written to be memorized and recited,
hence the measured prose. Mrs. Barbauld states in the
"Preface" that she chose prose because she did not wish to
lower poetry to the capacity of children. Rousseau, on the
hand, felt poetry was fine for amusing children but not for
teaching them. This memory work is in opposition to Rousseau's ideas also. Yet at the same time, both were opposed
to memorizing maxims. Mrs. Barbauld, however, allows
those when teaching the child to talk. [16]

In regard to Rousseau's negative education, or teaching virtue by not exposing the child to vice, Mrs. Barbauld's
child learns it is wrong to be a coward, learns to be kind to

animals and to share with people less fortunate. Mrs. Barbauld teaches these virtues, which Rousseau would not permit before the child is twelve.

There are a number of other points upon which the
two educators agree, but as Mrs. Barbauld does not mention
them in her books for children, I shall not discuss them.
One final point deserves mention, however; that is, Mrs.
Barbauld believed as Rousseau did, in the child's learning by
example whenever possible; she did not believe that any a-
mount of learning could determine what ultimately happens to
the child when he grows up. Mrs. Barbauld then believed
that Providence can and often does take over the child after
his father has finished with him. Providence may correct
bad habits in him which his father could not.[17] Rousseau
would insist that the child properly taught would not develop
bad habits, nor would Fortune be able to sway him. I believe Rousseau designed his Emile et Sophie to show Emile's
subsequent victory over the events which Providence had in
store for him.

A more detailed examination of Hymns in Prose reveals that although Mrs. Barbauld agreed with Rousseau often, especially in regard to the education of girls, she did
not follow him to any extent in the Hymns written for young
children with a distinctly religious purpose. For that reason
the only character pictured to any extent is God, whom she
pictures as the Creator of all nature. As Creator, He is to
be worshipped. The difference between man and the other
creatures is that man can worship. As the child grows older, he can praise God better (7); but even as a child he has
reason and hence can use it to praise God. Rousseau will
not admit that the child has the power to reason until he is
considerably older than the children for whom the Hymns
were written.

The God of the Hymns is not personified in nature,
but He is definitely easier to comprehend by the child because of Mrs. Barbauld's so stressing His hand in everyday
objects. For example, in Hymn 5, she teaches the child that
even at nighttime while the animals and the flowers retreat
into refreshing sleep, God watches over all (17-19). In
Hymn 9, God is invisible but His works are not. He is responsible for the flowers' and plants' knowing the season to
bloom. God never forgets, he sees all, knows all (33-37).

The lessons are simple in thought and often very beau-

tifully stated. Perhaps the above discussion implies that the
Hymns are didactic. They are, but not in the unattractive
sense which the word didactic carries. They can be quite
poetic; Hymn 2 is an example:

> Come, let us go forth into the fields
> let us see how the flowers spring,
> let us listen to the warbling of the birds,
> and sport ourselves upon the new grass.
>   The winter is over and gone,
> the birds come out upon the trees,
> the crimson blossoms of the peach and
> nectarine are seen,
> and the green leaves sprout.   (9)

Later this hymn goes into a discussion of young goslings,
chickens, and other animals; always praising God for everything, praise to which Rousseau did not want the child exposed.

      The subjects treated are, as Mrs. Barbauld promised,
everyday objects and events: the flowers, the trees, the animals, the seasons, the fields and the meadows, the day and
the night. In the hymn on family life, Hymn 8, she explains
how each person is a member of a family, families make up
towns, towns make up countries, countries make up kingdoms,
and God governs all (28-30). She continues the hymn with
an episode of a Negro woman in captivity who has a sick
child. God sees that child even if no one else does (30-31).
Mrs. Barbauld may have included this episode to teach the
child compassion for another race or to show him that all
races are under God's care. On the other hand, if those
were not the reasons, it is the only jarring note beyond the
understanding of children; that is, if it were meant to show
that God will take care of that Negro child because no white
person will, then it is a bit of social criticism which seems
misplaced in a book for children this young. Day and other
children's writers included social criticism, but their books
are written for older children.

      One of the most interesting hymns because of its sub-
ject and treatment of that subject is Hymn 10 on mortality.
The child learns to accept death. Mrs. Barbauld writes:

> Death is in the world, the
> spoiler is among the works of God.
> All that is made, must be destroyed;

all that is born must die:
let me alone, for I will weep yet longer. (40)

In Hymn 11 she continues this theme. She says she has
seen the dead flower and insect come alive again, so shall
it be with man. Jesus comes to help everyone live again:
"Child of immortality! mourn no longer" (42). Since Rousseau does not want the child exposed to religion, he never
discusses with Emile the subjects of immortality and death.

It is interesting that both writers are fond of analogy.
Mrs. Barbauld uses it frequently. She says in Hymn 12 that
life is good but death must come, the rose is beautiful, but
it has thorns (43-46). In Hymn 4 she describes the full
blown rose as beautiful and the lion as strong and the sun as
glorious. But God is more beautiful, stronger, and more
glorious (15-16).

The comparison with Rousseau is difficult because he
is very vague in Emile about the lessons of the first five
years. There can be little doubt that he would disagree with
the fundamental idea behind Hymns in Prose since he wished
to delay all concepts of God until Emile was at least eighteen. If the work had not been directed toward praise of God
through an understanding and appreciation of His creations,
then Rousseau probably would have approved of it, for he had
the same love of nature that is evidenced here. Rousseau's
influence exerts itself much more strongly in Mrs. Barbauld
and John Aikin's Evenings at Home.

Evenings at Home

Mrs. Barbauld's brother, John Aikin, a medical doc-
tor, collaborated with her on what became the most popular
of his works, Evenings at Home.[18] Dr. Aikin and his sister
were very fond of each other, so fond that Mrs. Barbauld
even persuaded Dr. Aikin to give his third son, Charles, to
her and her husband. Just as she wrote Lessons for Children for Charles, so Aikin wrote his part of Evenings at
Home for his two youngest children, Edmund and Lucy. Both
were educated entirely at home, according to Lucy,[19] a fact
which proves both Aikin and Mrs. Barbauld agreed with
Rousseau that parents should teach their own children. Aikin
was not as rigid as Rousseau in having a male teacher for
boys and a female for girls, for Aikin not only undertook the
education of Lucy, but also he wrote a number of father-

daughter dialogues in Evenings at Home. Papa and Sophie
discuss the value of animals in "What Animals are Made For"
and Papa and Cecilia discuss the meaning of emblems in "On
Emblems." The most extensive of the father-daughter dialogues are the three Papa-Lucy stories: "Why an Apple
Falls," "Why the Earth Moves Around the Sun," and "A Globe
Lecture."

Mrs. Barbauld also did not take Rousseau seriously
on having mothers educate daughters only, for she undertook
the education of Charles; however, in her contributions to
Evenings at Home,20 fourteen of the ninety-eight selections,
she has four which are father-son, not mother-son, dialogues:
"Things by Their Right Names," "On Manufactures," "A Lesson in the Art of Distinguishing," and "The Manufacture of
Paper."

Aikin wrote a number of father-son dialogues and a
series of nine tutor-George-Harry stories, all of which involve botany in some way. Aikin was extremely interested
in a number of subjects in Evenings at Home and in his other
writings; in addition to books on botany and medicine, he
wrote essays on biography, literary criticism, relations with
other countries, various aspects of the nature of man, such
as character formation, family pride, imitative principles,
and many others. As far as education is concerned, one
critic exclaims that John Aikin was "strongly influenced" by
the educational ideas of Rousseau, but she offers no support-
ing evidence other than the fact that Aikin believed in teaching by giving object lessons, not by having his children learn
by rote.21 Certainly in this idea he agrees with Rousseau.

Did Aikin read Emile? The question is a difficult
one. It seems most probable that he did. The reasons for
believing that he did read Emile are numerous: (1) He knew
The Confessions well; he wrote about them in his essay "On
Self-Biography"; (2) he knew La Nouvelle Héloise, for he
quoted part to his sister in a letter in 1787; (3) he knew
Rousseau's work Letters on Botany; (4) his sister had definitely read Emile, and as the two were very close, she probably discussed it with him; (5) he was extremely interested
in the education of children; (6) he had read Sandford and
Merton which, as indicated in Chapter III, relies heavily
on Emile, and (7) his own ideas on the education of boys
closely parallel Rousseau's.

Certainly John Aikin's ideas about the education of

women do not parallel Rousseau's, for Dr. Aikin definitely
had a more enlightened view of the role of women. He felt
they could and should be educated in more subjects than
those which involve housekeeping and caring for children.
While he believed that the most important characteristics of
a wife were her ability as a helper and as a companion,[22]
he distinguished between companion and plaything of men. In
general, he agreed with Rousseau that both sexes should be
educated according to what was likely to be the objects and
pursuits of their later lives. Lucy Aikin best describes the
beliefs of Aikin:

> But whatever kind of knowledge promised to be a
> permanent source of advantage worldly or moral,
> or of innocent and respectable amusement, he
> wished to be freely imparted to women as well as
> men; nor did I ever hear him express a doubt of
> their capacity for excelling in any branch of litera-
> ture or science. He loved female talent, and al-
> ways treated its possessors with distinguished re-
> spect and kindness.[23]

Dr. Aikin and Rousseau agreed that boarding schools
were, in general, undesirable. Aikin did feel, however,
that if the parent were not capable, for one reason or another, of teaching his own child, a boarding school might be
necessary.[24] This unfavorable attitude toward boarding
schools of the period appears to have been fairly generally
held.[25]

As Rousseau recognized the fact that the child who
desired to learn would get the best results, so Aikin recognized that knowledge in a palatable form is more easily di-
gested. In the "Introduction" to Evenings at Home, Aikin explains his plan. Mr. and Mrs. Fairborne encourage their
children to write fables or stories suitable for other young
people.[26] These are collected and kept in a box. On holi-
days when all assemble together, one child draws out a story
for them to read and discuss; another is then drawn and so
on until the evening has been spent in profitable amusement.[27]

No doubt these stories were profitable and amusing
when written,[28] for they even hold some charm today,[29] but
in regard to character development, the brevity of the stories
prohibits much in that line; consequently, Rousseau's influence on character is slight. Indur, of "The Transmigration

of Indur," is one of the most vivid characters, perhaps because his story is imaginative. Indur is a Brachman, who
is described in some detail (63), but never better than by
the story of how he saves a little monkey from a serpent's
bite at the cost of his own life. The little monkey is actually the fairy Perezinda[30] in disguise, who offers to grant
him one wish, although she has not the power to reverse the
poison of the serpent's bite. Indur wishes:

> In all my transmigrations may I retain a rational
> soul, with the memory of the adventures I have
> gone through; and when death sets me free from
> one body, may I instantly animate another, in the
> prime of its powers and faculties, without passing
> through the helpless state of infancy. (63)

Indur retains his nobility and generous nature as he becomes
in turn an antelope, a wild goose, a dormouse, an elephant,
a whale, a bee, a rabbit, and finally a mastiff. In this last
state, he gives his life willingly to save his master who accidentally shoots him. He dies licking his grieving master's
hand; and awakening again, he finds himself in his native
land, a Brachman again. The reason for his return to human form, according to Aikin, is that "so generous a nature
was now no longer to be annexed to a brutal form" (74).
This story shows generosity being rewarded, but as Indur had
no idea he would be rewarded for his actions, I believe Indur
exhibits that true generosity which Rousseau advocated.

The character whom Rousseau appears to have influenced most is William in "Eyes and No Eyes." The plot is
simple: William and Robert both take a walk. Upon their
return, Mr. Andrews inquires about what they have seen.
Robert has seen almost nothing; William has seen a great
deal because he used his eyes. He has discovered mistletoe,
a green woodpecker (an English parrot), three kinds of heath,
a wheat-ear (a grayish bird), a flock of lapwings, a viper,
fifteen church-steeples, a water rat, a kingfisher, sand-
pipers, sand-martins, a man spearing eels, a heron, some
starlings, some clods of marle which were full of sea-shells,
the clouds and sun. All of these items arouse the curiosity
of William who questions Mr. Andrews and thereby learns
much of nature (213-19). Most important, is the fact that he
learns from a desire on his own part.

There are several female characters who are educated
much as Rousseau's Sophie is. One is Kitty, who appears

with Mamma in "Dialogues on Things to be Learned." Kitty learns the importance of education to fit people for their station in life, of marketing, of looking after the servants and children, of reading and writing, of knowing some geography, of some knowledge of plants, animals, heavenly bodies, history, French, and dancing. Music and drawing are more ornamental accomplishments (37-42). The difference between the education of Kitty and the education of Sophie lies in the additional information given to Kitty about astronomy, history, geography, and botany which Rousseau would not find necessary for a girl's education. Little Sally Meanwell is another female character who, like Sophie, accepts her position in life in "A Dialogue on Different Stations in Life" (23-27).

The character of the tutor appears to be modeled after Rousseau's tutor. He knows the answer to all questions asked of him, and he is with the boys whenever they have a question. The tutor in Evenings at Home is represented by different people: the mother, the father, Mr. Andrews, Mr. Barlow, and the tutor of George and Harry. Some of these tutors are not quite so talented as Rousseau's tutor when it comes to resisting a lecture. They often teach by story and example rather than by experience, as Rousseau advocated.

There are characters of fairies in two cases, Perezinda who gives Indur his wish and the fairies, Disorder and Order, who contrive to get Juliet in and out of trouble in the story "Order and Disorder, a Fairy Tale" (290-300). It was the opinion of Rousseau and many others that fairy tales were bad for children. Dr. Aikin would appear to have quieted some of his opponents' criticism by making his fairy tale teach a most obvious lesson. 31 Thus a number of characters are in the tradition of Rousseau, but Aikin is far from a slave to that tradition.

There is no real plot in Evenings at Home; 32 there is simply a series of stories, some of which result from the tutor's contriving a situation which will lead to questions and answers. The nine tutor-George-Harry stories are an example; they are "On the Oak," "On the Pine and Fir Tribe," "The Grass Tribe," "On Wine and Spirits," "The Leguminous Plants," "The Umbelliferous Plants," "On Earth and Stones," "The Cruciform-flowered Plants," and "The Compound-flowered Plants."

There are situations resulting from some everyday

incidents which generally lead to a parent-child dialogue.
That Rousseau used dialogues between the tutor and Emile is
no proof that he influenced Aikin and Barbauld in this respect; yet it is another way in which the three are similar.
I have named most of the father-daughter dialogues earlier,
as well as the father-son ones written by Mrs. Barbauld.
Dr. Aikin also wrote father-son dialogues and even mother-
daughter ones. A brief look at the subjects of these will
show how they arose, supposedly, from an everyday event.
"Half-a-Crown's Worth" is primarily a letter in answer to a
son's wish for a larger allowance. The letter consists of
listing the truly important or essential things which could be
purchased with the half-a-crown that the son would foolishly
waste (139-41). "On Presence of Mind"33 is a dialogue between Mrs. F. and Eliza. The occasion is Mrs. F.'s being
bled; Eliza does not wish to watch, but her mother insists.
She must get accustomed to little things like the sight of
blood if she is to keep her presence of mind when serious
accidents occur. She will not run or not know what to do;
she may save a life one day by her presence of mind (154-
60). Rousseau would probably have admired presence of
mind in Sophie, but he does not mention it.

Other stories arise from other common situations. A
good bit of chemistry is to be learned from "A Tea Lecture"
(87-91). A visit to various churches on Sunday makes vivid
the differences among religions in "Difference and Agreement;
or Sunday Morning" (222-24). This list could go on and on;
a look at the overall plan of the book, however, would be
more beneficial for showing some points about plot and Rousseau's effect on it not previously mentioned.

The structure of Evenings at Home is based upon
small groups of various readings to provide an evening's en-
tertainment. The six volumes of 1792-1796 were in the
nineteenth century combined into one volume, divided into
readings for thirty evenings. There is variety in each evening's group; for example, the first evening's reading contains a dialogue, two fables,34 and a story of a traveler; the
second evening's reading contains a drama, a story told from
the point of view of a squirrel, a dialogue, an allegory, a
fairy tale, and a poem.35

Although fables and poems very often have some plot,
these do not have much in that line. Many stories told from
the point of view of animals merely recall one incident after
another in their lives, as do the stories of travelers. The

dramas have some semblance of plot, but as they are extremely short, they have about as much plot as the modern
one-act play. Rousseau's influence on these fables and dramas seems neglibible.

      The plot of one story, however, may be influenced by
Rousseau. The story, "Trial,"[36] has a well-constructed
plot; Dr. Aikin describes the story as "Of a Complaint made
against sundry persons for breaking the Windows of Dorothy
Careful, Widow, and Dealer in Gingerbread" (142).

      Henry Luckless is falsely accused of throwing the
stone which broke Widow Careful's window. The judge hears
both sides of the case. New evidence appears in the form
of a top with the initials P. R. cut into it. The court ad-
journs, and the public treasurer pays the widow; however, a
court of inquiry investigates Peter Riot and his friends. The
members of the court question Tom Frisk and Bob Loiter and
discover the motive for the crime: Widow Careful would not
let Peter have any more gingerbread until he paid his debt
of a sixpence. More new evidence is introduced in the form
of a shoe buckle found near the scene of the crime. Then
the condemning fact becomes clear: Peter Riot has his
shoes tied with strings now. Before the trial, Peter thinks
it best to confess, so he pays a half-crown to the public
treasury and makes a public apology to Widow Careful (142-
49). Thus his punishment is befitting his crime. Rousseau's
idea of crime and punishment serves as the foundation for
the story's beginning, middle and end, and accounts in part
for its conflict and denouement.

      As he does not often concern himself with plot, Dr.
Aikin commits on one occasion that great sin to a master of
plot--the deus ex machina. In "The Power of Habit" two
brothers, James and Richard, grow up in completely different ways: James is accustomed to every indulgence; Richard, on the other hand, is accustomed to plain living and
working and acquiring useful knowledge. Richard appears to
be following Rousseau's advice. When the boys' father dies,
leaving them with little money, Richard by his industry
makes his way and lives a modest, but happy, life. James,
however, gambles and loses what little he has. He accepts
a position in a regiment, setting off for the West Indies
(303-306). To prove that James could not change and improve
his ways, Aikin simply eliminates the problem of James by
having him die of a fever shortly after his arrival in the
West Indies. Rousseau's tutor who contrived and deceived in

order to prove a point to his pupil probably would not have
objected to the use of the deus ex machina for such a worthy
purpose; on the other hand, the deus ex machina does not
fit in with Rousseau's idea of punishment fitting the crime.
Perhaps a more fitting end for James would have been a bul-
let from the gun of an enraged gambler whom James had
tried to cheat.

Rousseau and Aikin did not agree on other points,
such as the use of fables and fairies and the stating of the
moral. On the other hand, Aikin treats subjects of a social
and political nature; for example, he expresses his views on
war in "The Price of Victory" and "The Cost of a War."
Rousseau felt strongly that the child needed assistance to become a good and useful citizen.

There are numerous subjects treated in Evenings at
Home that result from a child's observations of nature--
trees, birds, fish, animals, and people of all kinds. Dr.
Aikin's interest in botany coincided with Rousseau's interest.
Aikin also taught his children and readers about the building
of ships, the characteristics of metals, the life in the colon-
ies, the nature of men, the differences in various religions.
Also generosity, friendship, respect for others, self-reliance
are the themes of several of Aikin's and Mrs. Barbauld's stories.

Aikin uses a technique of building one lesson upon another. He continues a subject and develops it so that the
child remembers the earlier lesson, and he generally has
enough interest to want to hear more about the topic. Specifically, Aikin writes continued stories on the results of war,
on metals, on various plants, on a study of gravity and various relationships between the earth and the universe. Rousseau also felt the interest of the child or the child's desire
to learn must be cultivated.

Thus, both Mrs. Barbauld and Dr. Aikin were very
much aware of Rousseau, but she more than her brother,
chose to ignore much of Rousseau's teachings. Both believed
the child could have knowledge at a younger age than Rousseau permitted. Aikin allowed female education to include
more knowledge than either Rousseau or Mrs. Barbauld allowed.
All three preferred to teach by experience, but Aikin and Mrs.
Barbauld did use other methods; Rousseau did not. A love
of nature is common to all three, as it is to Thomas Day
who, much more than Aikin and Mrs. Barbauld, felt Rousseau's
impact on his thinking and writing.

Notes

1. Anna Laetitia Barbauld, The Works of Anna Laetitia Barbauld, with a Memoir by Lucy Aikin (2 vols.; London:
   Longman, 1825), I, lxvii. Miss Aikin also points out
   that this essay first appeared in the Monthly Magazine.

2. Ibid., II, 309.

3. For detailed information on famous pupils and on subjects
   taught, see Barbauld, I, xxv-xxxiii.

4. Barbauld, p. xix. Miss Aikin tells the occasion when
   Mrs. Barbauld made this statement, but not to whom
   she made the statement.

5. Ibid., p. xvii-xviii.

6. Ibid., p. xix-xx.

7. Cornelia Lynde Meigs, "Roots in the Past up to 1840,"
   A Critical History of Children's Literature: A Survey
   of Children's Books in English from Earliest Times to
   the Present, Prepared in 4 pts., ed. Cornelia L.
   Meigs (New York: Macmillan, 1953), p. 94.

8. Anna Laetitia Barbauld, "Advertisement by the Author,"
   Lessons for Children, from Two to Four Years Old
   (Philadelphia: B. F. Bache, 1788). The editor in
   "Advertisement by the Editor" of this edition claims
   that in teaching her own children to read, she used
   these books; and her children not only read them perfectly in a very short time, but the experience also
   enabled them to read perfectly in any book.

9. Charles Lamb, as cited by Montrose Jonas Moses, Children's Books and Reading (New York: Mitchell Kennerley, 1907), p. 99.

10. Charles Lamb, as cited by Paul Hazard, Books, Chil-
    dren, and Men, trans. Marguerite Mitchell (Boston:
    The Horn Book, Inc., 1944), p. 33.

11. Part I, p. 15-19. All further references to this work
    will be indicated by the page numbers in parentheses
    in the body of the text.

12. This story is included in Forgotten Tales of Long Ago,
     selected by E. V. Lucas (London: Wells, Gardner,
     Darton and Co., 1906).

13. (Boston: S. Hall, 1800).

14. Anna Laetitia Barbauld, Hymns in Prose for Children
     (4th ed.; Norwich: Printed, by John Trumbull,
     1786), p. iv-v. All future references to this work
     will be indicated by the page numbers in parentheses
     in the body of the text.

15. F. J. Harvey Darton, Children's Books in England:
     Five Centuries of Social Life (Cambridge at the Uni-
     versity Press, 1932), p. 54, points out this agree-
     ment and yet disagreement also. So does Bess Por-
     ter Adams, About Books and Children: Historical
     Survey of Children's Literature (New York: Henry
     Holt and Co., Inc., 1953), p. 52; and Florence V.
     Barry, A Century of Children's Books (New York:
     George H. Doran Co., 1923), p. 149.

16. Barbauld, Works, II, 307.

17. Ibid., p. 319.

18. John Aikin and Anna Laetitia Barbauld, Evenings at
     Home; or, The Juvenile Budget Opened: Consisting
     of a Variety of Miscellaneous Pieces for the Instruc-
     tion and Amusement of Young Persons (Edinburgh:
     William P. Nimmo, n.d.). Because of the type of
     illustration included and because of the modern "s"
     used, I would definitely date this edition in the nine-
     teenth century. It is dated ca. 1830 in John Mackay
     Shaw, Childhood in Poetry: A Catalogue (5 vols.;
     Detroit: Gale Research Co., 1967), I, 20.

19. Lucy Aikin, Memoir of John Aikin, M.D. (Philadelphia:
     Abraham Small, 1824), p. 93-94.

20. Her contributions, according to Lucy Aikin in Works,
     I, xxxvi-xxxviin. are "The Young Mouse;" "The Wasp
     and Bee;" "Alfred, a drama;" "Animals and Coun-
     tries;" "Canute's Reproof;" "The Masque of Nature;"
     "Things by Their Right Names;" "The Goose and
     Horse;" "On Manufactures;" "The Flying-fish;" "A
     Lesson in the Art of Distinguishing;" "The Phoenix

and Dove;" "The Manufacture of Paper;" and "The
Four Sisters." Meigs, p. 76, refers to these stories
as prosaic, with no vision of the world of children's
imaginations. I disagree with this criticism especially in regard to "Things by Their Right Names."

21. Betsy Rodgers, Georgian Chronicle: Mrs. Barbauld
    and Her Family (London: Methuen, 1958), p. 124.

22. John Aikin, "Choice of a Wife," as cited by Lucy Aikin,
    Memoir, p. 99.

23. Ibid., p. 100.

24. It must be remembered that his sister and her husband
    ran a boarding school for eleven years.

25. Some of the reasons for this attitude are seen in the
    discussion in Chapter VI of Dorothy Kilner's Anec-
    dotes of a Boarding-School.

26. A similar plan is used by Lady Eleanor Fenn in The
    Juvenile Tatler, discussed in Chapter VI.

27. Evenings at Home, p. 5. All future references to this
    work will be indicated by the page numbers in paren-
    theses in the body of the text.

28. The book enjoyed a warm reception. For further in-
    formation on its reception, see Austin Dobson, "The
    Parent's Assistant," DeLibris: Prose and Verse
    (New York: Macmillan, 1908), p. 123.

29. That the book still holds some interest is evident from
    the fact that my eleven-year-old neighbor enjoyed
    a number of the stories.

30. Obviously Aikin disregarded Rousseau's objection to
    fairies here.

31. Annie E. Moore, Literature Old and New for Children
    (Boston: Houghton Mifflin Co., 1934), p. 187,
    states that there are no real fairy tales in Evenings
    at Home. The magical powers of Perezinda, how-
    ever, seem to contradict her statement.

32. Darton, p. 158, points out that the weakness of the

moral tale is in its construction.

33. This story is cited in Gillian Elise Avery, Nineteenth
    Century Children: Heroes and Heroines in English
    Children's Stories, 1780-1900 (London: Hodder and
    Stoughton, 1965), p. 213, as an illustration of the
    "Georgian Awful Example," a brief and pithy story
    giving stark facts with no sentimentality. I agree
    with Miss Avery completely.

34. Meigs, p. 89, discusses the term fable and says: "As
    a truly fanciful story [the fable] was condemned, as
    an allegory presenting vague personifications
    of good and evil, the right way and wrong way, it
    was hesitatingly approved." The latter describes the
    fables of Evenings at Home.

35. That Aikin and Barbauld included poetry when their pur-
    pose was to amuse and instruct is in opposition to
    Rousseau's view of poetry, which was merely to de-
    light.

36. This story is included in Old-Fashioned Tales, selected
    by E. V. Lucas (London: Wells, Gardner, Darton
    and Co. , 1905).

Chapter III

Thomas Day

The impact of Rousseau's Emile upon Thomas Day
was definitely greater than upon any other writer being considered here. For that reason, more critics have pointed
out and described this influence than they have Rousseau's
effect upon the other writers. Their comments will be summarized in the following pages and attention will be paid to
some influences which have hitherto been overlooked.

The biographer of Day, George W. Gignilliat, quotes
the preface to the original edition of Sandford and Merton in
which Day states his purpose as providing children with reading suitable for them, reading which would both form and interest their minds. Day continued, "from their applause
alone I shall estimate my success."[1] Mrs. Barbauld's Lessons and Edgeworth's Harry and Lucy influenced Day. He
actually began Sandford and Merton as a short story to be
included in Harry and Lucy.[2] It grew and grew, however,
taking novel form and being published in three separate volumes in 1783, 1786, and 1789.[3]

Because Day was so concerned with children's opinions
and with writing for children, his work is easily distinguished
from that of Henry Brooke who wrote the Fool of Quality,
which has been called a "novelized Emile." The Fool of
Quality was not written to be read by children any more than
Emile was; yet it influenced Day in both his choice of character and his choice of incident.[4] Day then was influenced
by Rousseau's ideas both directly from his readings of Emile
and indirectly from Brooke's novel. Furthermore, Day met
and talked with Rousseau himself, prior to his writing of
Sandford and Merton. The man who said in a letter to
Edgeworth in 1769 that he valued Emile second only to the
Bible,[5] was understandably willing to accompany Edgeworth
and Edgeworth's oldest son, Richard, still a child under
eight, to Paris to have the youth examined by Rousseau. He
had been reared by his father as closely as possible to Rousseau's principles set forth in Emile. The results of this

meeting will be discussed in the chapter on Maria Edgeworth.

Day himself was to conduct an experiment along the
lines set forth by Rousseau. It is mentioned briefly here to
show that Day was truly a disciple of Rousseau, as appears
plainly in his two books for children, Sandford and Merton
and The History of Little Jack. The experiment also shows
that Rousseau's ideas were put to use better in books than
in real life. Day decided to educate two young orphan girls
in the manner of Rousseau with the ultimate intention of making one his wife. Surely the picture of the devoted, gentle
helpmate and companion, Sophie, would appeal to any man.
Day, however, had not met any Sophies; unlike Emile, he
was having trouble meeting a woman who would share a belief in plain dress, country life, hard work, and most of all,
who would accept his lack of grace in dancing and lack of
social polish. Edgeworth's sister Margaret, after being en-
gaged to Day and after a separation period (in the manner of
Emile and Sophie), rejected Day and broke the engagement.
Day was discouraged and terribly disappointed until he came
upon the idea of educating a Sophie for himself rather than
trying to acquire grace and polish to make himself attractive
to the opposite sex.

To educate a Sophie was Day's goal when he went to
the orphanage and took two girls whom he named Sabrina
Sidney and Lucretia. Sabrina was twelve, a year older than
Lucretia. He set about teaching them to hate finery of all
kinds, as well as all class distinctions. Gignilliat claims
that the subjects taught to the girls were based on Rousseau's
teaching, but Day impressed these subjects upon the girls in
a manner uncharacteristic of Rousseau: "continual talk, ab-
struse reasoning, and ridicule."[6]

By 1770, one year after choosing the girls, Day gave
up Lucretia; he found her too stupid for his plans. She became an apprentice to a chamber milliner, and he gave her
three or four hundred pounds upon her marriage to a linen-
draper--all according to his original plan which he had presented to the orphanage. Lucretia lived a contented life.[7]

Sabrina, on the other hand, had to submit to Day's
application of some of Rousseau's ideas intended for the education of men. Specifically, Rousseau said a child should be
accustomed to the sound of firearms. Rousseau also said,
in speaking of savages, that they should be accustomed to
burns, so they will not be slaves to pain. When Day fired

a pistol, minus the ball, close to Sabrina's ear and when he
poured hot sealing wax upon her arms, Sabrina failed to re-
act as Day felt she should. He sent her to boarding school.
At sixteen when she was staying at the house of a friend of
Day's, she failed to wear the precise uniform or dress which
Day advocated for her. As a result, Day felt she had
changed her attitude toward him, and he left her permanently.
She went to live in a boarding house on fifty pounds a year
until she was almost thirty. At that time she married Mr.
Bicknell, a friend of Day's, a man in failing health. He
died three years later in 1787, leaving Sabrina with two boys.
Friends of his provided for her, and Day continued to give
her thirty pounds a year. [8]

The History of Sandford and Merton

     The experiment was a failure, but Day never com-
pletely lost faith in Rousseau's ideals for education. Proof
appears in Sandford and Merton in the character of Miss
Simmons whom Day obviously patterned after Sabrina. Miss
Sukey Simmons is the only one who befriends Harry Sandford,
the farmer's son, when he goes to the house of the wealthy
Merton family. She is the only one who overlooks, or does
not even consider, Harry's lower social standing. Miss
Simmons' drawing room talent is reading didactic and educational stories, not playing dull music that almost puts the
audience to sleep. In fact, Miss Simmons is in the tradition
of Sophie; she has never been sickly nor pampered, for her
uncle who raised her had evidently read Emile. Day says:

> [Miss Simmons] was accustomed from her earliest
> years to plunge into the cold bath at every season
> of the year, to rise by candlelight in winter, to
> ride a dozen miles upon a trotting horse, or to
> walk as many, even with the hazard of being
> splashed, or of soiling her clothes. By this mode
> of education, Miss Sukey (for so she had the mis-
> fortune to be named) acquired an excellent charac-
> ter, accompanied, however, with some dispositions
> which disqualified her almost as much as Harry for
> fashionable life. She was acquainted with all the
> best authors in our own language, nor was she ig-
> norant of those in French, although she could not
> speak a word of the language. [There was no need
> to learn French since Miss Sukey's uncle expected
> her to marry an Englishman and live in England.][9]

Also like Sophie, Sukey is to learn all household tasks. But going a step further than Rousseau, Day permits Sukey a knowledge of the laws of nature and the fundamentals of geometry (253). Unlike Rousseau, Day did not care for music much, the performance or appreciation of it being one of those infernal social graces. Rousseau, of course, loved music and even developed his own theory of writing music which he planned to teach Sophie; Day permits Sukey a few songs but no study of music (253). The episode mentioned earlier in which the audience dies of boredom indicates Day's true feelings about music, for Harry even falls asleep during the playing of music at the Mertons' house one evening.

Miss Sukey Simmons is without doubt the most admirable female in Sandford and Merton. She is understanding, kind, good-natured, friendly, and even sympathetic when the occasion calls for such a nature. Day clearly modeled her character after Sophie; but the character modeled after Emile is not so clearcut; that is, both Tommy Merton and Harry Sandford possess some of Emile's characteristics. It is true that Harry appears to be much closer to Emile in his actions and beliefs, but it is significant that Emile is a gentleman; and in Sandford and Merton, it is Tommy who is the gentleman. Also Day makes it plain that Tommy is basically a good-natured, generous lad; it is his lack of the proper kind of education, as well as his lack of the proper surroundings and companionship, that causes all his problems. Like Emile, Tommy is the protagonist of his novel. The title of the novel suggests it is the story of two boys as indeed it is, but Harry's main function is to show the right way to behave and to serve as a good example for Tommy.

Harry has two advantages over Tommy. First, he is a farmer's boy, and, as such, he is infinitely better than a gentleman's boy in Day's opinion. Day paints black and white characters with the rich being no good and the poor being all good.[10] Mr. Merton, Tommy's father, has his moments of goodness and understanding, but he is the only gray character that Day lets slip into the novel. The second advantage Harry has over Tommy is that he has been under the care of Mr. Barlow longer. He already knows much of what Tommy learns; thus both Harry and Mr. Barlow serve as tutors for Tommy.

Day closely patterns the character of Mr. Barlow after the tutor of Emile. Both Harry and Tommy are sent to live with Mr. Barlow; thus he is with them all day; and

while he is ever-present, he is also all-knowing. When he
and Tommy are apart, Tommy regresses; hence Day evidently felt the tutor should always be there as Rousseau said he
should. Mr. Barlow's main principle is one taken from
Rousseau, but taken to extremes; that is, people are to be
judged by their usefulness. Everything and everybody must
be useful. The poor who produce most of the food of the
land, and the clothing, and the shelter--they are the citizens
to admire. The rich have only gold and finery which will
get them nowhere if they are ever isolated and marooned on
a desert island (342-44). The difference then between Day
and Rousseau is that Rousseau wanted to prepare Emile for
any change in fortune which might occur, but Day wants his
pupils to be able to survive and even enjoy life on a desert
island. It would seem that Rousseau is the more practical
of the two.[11]

Mr. Barlow teaches by experience and by lecture.
The latter method is not in keeping with Rousseau's method,
but it often makes for a more interesting story. Some of
Mr. Barlow's lectures merely preach morals; but some of
them involve Tommy's learning a moral from an interpolated
story. Sometimes Mr. Barlow finds it necessary to talk a-
bout the experiences of Tommy to make sure he learned the
proper lesson. One such lecture occurs when Day interrupts
an interpolated story, "Sophron and Tigranes." This story
contains some history, but it is the biography of the main
character that contains the desired lesson. Learning from
biography rather than history agrees with Rousseau's ideas
on the subject.

It is in the interpolated story "Sophron and Tigranes"
that the character of Chares appears (330). I do not believe
anyone has ever pointed out the similarities between this man
and Rousseau.[12] On the surface, it would seem they have
little in common. Chares is an orphan from a city in Asia;
he traveled a great deal; eventually he had a daughter whom
he is now interested in educating. Beneath the surface, it
seems that Chares in his travels in always careful to get to
know well the people of the country in which he travels, a
knowledge which Rousseau insists Emile acquire. At the time of
the story, a group of men are pursuing Chares. He is not
permitted to live the simple, country life without luxury that
he believes in. Chares wants to live close to nature. He
says: "He is happiest who passes his time in innocent em-
ployment and the observation of nature." He continues with
an appraisal of cities that echoes Rousseau's views: "I had

visited many of the principal cities in several countries
where I had travelled; but I had uniformly observed, that the
miseries and crimes of mankind increased with their numbers" (403).

Chares has an appreciation of nature that sounds deis-
tic as Rousseau sometimes sounds: Chares says: "I frequently observed, with admiration, the wisdom and contriv-
ance which were displayed in all the productions of nature,
and the perfection of all her works" (404). Chares, like
Rousseau, loves nature to the extent that he studies the soil
and the air in an effort to learn more about the growth of
plants. Rousseau, of course, had a lifelong interest in botany.

One final point of similarity is the interest in education which both men possess--Chares for the sake of his
daughter Selene; Rousseau, for every daughter's sake. Both
oppose false delicacy and what Chares calls "the useless
arts, which terminate in vanity and sensuality" (407).
Selene's activities are not unlike some of Sophie's:

> With the rising sun she left her bed, and accom-
> panied me to the garden or the vineyard. Her
> little hands were employed in shortening the lux-
> urious shoots of fruitful trees. . . . With what de-
> light did I view her innocent cheerfulness and as-
> siduity! With what pleasure did she receive the
> praises which I gave to her skill and industry; or
> hear the lessons of wisdom and the examples of
> virtuous women, which I used to read her in the
> evening, from the writings of celebrated philoso-
> phers, which I had collected in my travels. (408)

Rousseau does not mention gardening for Sophie; he
stresses indoor activities more, such as needlework. Yet
the two men are basically in agreement. Women need exercise. Rousseau does not want Emile to learn by having
stories read to him, but he is less particular about Sophie's
method of learning.

Chares is similar to Rousseau in another respect.
They both admire the man of simplicity, reared as Nature
would rear him. Chares meets such a man in the character
of Arsaces, the king of the Scythians; he describes his meeting with Arsaces:

> I was surprised at the vigour and penetration which
> I discovered in this untutored warrior's mind. Un-
> biased by the mass of prejudices which we acquire
> in cities, even from our earliest childhood, unen-
> cumbered by forms and ceremonies which contract
> the understanding while they pretend to improve the
> manners, he seemed to possess a certain energy
> of soul that never missed the mark. Nature in
> him had produced the same effects that study and
> philosophy do in others. . . . He entertained a
> rooted contempt for all the arts that soften the
> body and mind, under the pretense of adding to the
> elegancies of life; these, he said, were more ef-
> ficacious agents to reduce men to slavery, than the
> swords and arrows of their enemies." (418)

This is a person who appears to be the kind of man Rousseau
would have Emile be.

Rousseau, then, definitely influenced the characters;
the plot, on the other hand, shows less evidence of Rousseau's influence. The plot is haphazard at best. The only
unifying element is Tommy. Since it is Tommy who must
learn, the novel revolves around his lessons, whether they
be in the form of exercise, experience, lecture, dialogue,
moralizing, or interpolated story. Both Emile and Sandford
and Merton are vehicles for their authors' ideas rather than
carefully plotted novels; but regardless of the lack of plot,
a number of episodes are quite similar.

Day borrowed from Emile the episode about the magnet. Emile and his tutor went to the fair where they saw a
man make a wax duck follow a piece of bread around. 13
Tommy, along with Harry and Mr. Barlow, happens to see a
performer whistle to a little toy swan. Upon being ordered
to come, the swan swims across a basin to the hand of its master
in which there is a piece of bread (219). In both cases the
boys learn about magnets as a result.

Another incident borrowed from Emile is the vivid
way in which Emile learns about astronomy; when he is lost,
he uses his knowledge of astronomy to get home again.
Harry tells Tommy that once when he was lost in the woods,
he had to find his way home by consulting the constellation
of Charles's Wain and the Polestar (177).

When Tommy first went to live with Mr. Barlow, an

incident occurred which is similar to Emile's learning of the
rights of property when he dug up the Maltese melons to
plant his beans. The purpose of Day's gardening lesson is
different, however, for Tommy learns the value of usefulness
rather than respect for the property of others. Tommy does
not wish to work in the garden, for he is a gentleman, not a
farmer. After Harry and Mr. Barlow finish their gardening,
they eat ripe cherries. Tommy expects his share, but he
soon learns that he will not get any until he does his part of
the work (13-14).

Tommy and Emile both learn to read because their
creators contrive situations in which the boys express a desire to learn. Rousseau is vague on this point, merely saying that if no one is avilable to read to Emile his invitations
and he misses a few events this way, he will soon learn to
read. Day has Harry, who can read, go home for a week.
As a result, Tommy hears no stories and wants to, so he
asks Harry, upon the latter's return, to teach him (23-24).
Gignilliat notes that Tommy is six or a little older; whereas
Emile is fifteen. Tommy at that age is encouraged in the
development of his sensibility and religious nature; whereas
Emile must wait another ten years for such encouragement.[14]

Rousseau and Day had similar beliefs about punishment. The crime should dictate the punishment. This idea
often determines the plot, for when a crime of a certain nature is committed, the punishment which inevitably follows
must be of the same nature. Gignilliat points out that Day
always rewards virtue while Rousseau looks upon virtue as
an end in itself.[15] This fact is true, and, as a consequence,
Day has to make his reward suit the good deed just as he
makes his punishment suit the bad deed. An example or two
will suffice to demonstrate how these actions affect the plot.
In the interpolated story "The Good-Natured Little Boy" (73-
89), a little boy who has all his food for the day in a basket
sets out for a walk to the village. He comes upon a poor
starving dog, so he offers the dog part of his food. The dog
continues with him, and they come upon a groaning horse.
Although afraid of not being able to make it home by dark,
the boy takes time to gather grass and water for the horse;
the horse is then able to rise and graze by himself. Then
the child chances upon a man in a pond; as he is a blind
man, he cannot seem to find his way out of the water. The
boy leads the blind man out, and then hurries off. Before
long he comes upon a hungry sailor who has lost both legs
and is, therefore, using crutches. The child then gives

away the remainder of his food.

   Now Day gives the child his reward. Darkness comes
upon him. He is lost, tired and hungry, so he sits down to
cry. All of a sudden the dog comes up with several slices
of meat and bread neatly wrapped in a handkerchief. Feeling somewhat refreshed after eating, the boy tries to find his
way again. He chances upon the horse whom he had fed.
The horse lets him mount and carries him to an opening in
the woods. As the youth is continuing on, two men jump on
him, intent upon stealing his clothes. His dog bites one and
diverts him from the boy. Suddenly help arrives--who, but
the legless sailor on the shoulders of the blind man. The
sailor had overheard the villains talk of robbing the boy.
Help comes to the boy as a reward, for he had tried to help
the others. Rousseau would praise this boy and Harry also,
for always trying to determine the cause of suffering, as
well as trying to alleviate it.

   The story of "The Ill-Natured Boy" (87-94), which follows almost immediately, is a good example of a story where
the punishment suits the crime. The boy of this story is the
son of a man who made no effort toward his son's education
and who had many bad habits which his child also developed.
The boy scatters a flock of sheep against a shepherd boy's
wish, he overturns a bucket of milk which a little girl is
carrying, he pushes several children playing ball into a ditch,
he affixes a bunch of thorns to a jackass's tail, he offers a
blind man part of his breakfast and pretending to direct him
has him sit down in a heap of wet dung, he pulls out the
stick a lame beggar was using to aid himself in walking.

   Then comes the justifiable punishment. He is caught
by a farmer stealing apples. The farmer's dog bites him;
the farmer whips him and upon learning that he is the very
boy who frightened his sheep that morning, he gives him an
extra thrashing. Then the boy falls into the hands of the
lame beggar who thrashes him even more with his stick. He
tries to get home, but he comes upon the group he had
pushed into the ditch. They torment him in various ways--
pinching him and pulling his hair, for example. Trying to
escape from those boys, he sees the jackass and jumps upon
its back. The shouts of the boys scare the animal and he
takes off. The ill-natured boy cries out for help after the
ass has thrown him to the ground and broken his leg. Who
should come to his assistance, but the little girl whose bucket of milk he had deliberately turned over. She, however,

is willing to repay a bad deed with a good one. She helps
him to her father's cottage. Both she and the events of the
day give him cause for reflection: he resolves to take every
opportunity for doing good in the future. In this manner then
do Day's ideas regarding reward and punishment govern plot.

The influence of Rousseau is not nearly so profound
upon plot as it is upon the themes or subjects treated in
Sandford and Merton. Both authors believed in no luxury of
any kind, Day perhaps being more insistent upon this point
than Rousseau, for Day has the climax of the novel occur
when Tommy changes his fine clothes for plain and simple
clothes (433). Day praises simplicity of taste in food in the
interpolated story "History of a Surprising Cure of the Gout"
(148-61). In regard to the eating of meat, which Rousseau
opposed, Gignilliat points out that Sophron, the hero of the
interpolated story "Sophron and Tigranes," refers to the fruits
of nature as more suitable nourishment than lambs.[16]

Both authors advocated exercise, hard work, and useful activity. Both Emile and Tommy learn about gardening
and a little about carpentry. Emile learns about the job of
a blacksmith; Tommy learns about the use of levers and of
wedges for chopping wood.

In addition to bodily development, both authors were
intent upon developing the mind and reasoning power of their
pupils. The subjects taught are often the same: astronomy,
history, geography. Day teaches these things to the youthful
Tommy, but Rousseau waits to teach them until Emile is older. Gignilliat notes the similarity between Tommy's learning about the telescope and Emile's learning about the re-
fractive power of water from a glass prism.[17]

Rousseau is adamant about no fairies or fables. No
fairies or fables appear in Day's works, but he does rely
upon legend a great deal. He uses stories of Lapland,
Greenland, ancient Sparta, Kamtschatka, Athens and others.
Both authors would have their pupils know about animals and
plants and people.

The development of virtue is of primary importance
in the philosophies of both Rousseau and Day. Both teach
generosity, although it is significant that Rousseau does not
want the child rewarded for generosity, for then it ceases to
be true generosity. Day is closer to Locke on this point;
both Day and Locke reward good-natured acts. A specific

example of virtue or good-natured action is kindness to animals. Day and Rousseau mention this point, but Day has more examples than Rousseau. Both teach their pupils to respect the rights and the property of others.

These rights bring up the relationship of the boy to society. Rousseau and Day would have their boys believe that there is a distinction between gentlemen and the lower classes, but that the upper class is not necessarily the good and the lower, the bad. In fact, as pointed out earlier, Day often pictures completely the reverse. He is merciless in his pictures of the selfish, inconsiderate rich boy or girl. Harry says to Mr. Barlow: "I generally observe, that they who are rich, will scarcely treat the poor with common civility" (397). Although the rich are so undesirable in many ways, Day has Mr. Barlow "unceasingly intent upon bringing the two classes nearer together" (245).

Both distinguish between other races and nationalities, again without condemning because of the difference. Day goes further than Rousseau in this regard and injects much social criticism of the treatment of the poor and some of the treatment of the Negro. The Negro incident is another example of plot being governed by Day's idea of restitution. Tommy and Harry and others are watching a bull-baiting (293). A poor Negro, hungry and in need of clothing, approaches them. Tommy has nothing to give, having previously spent all his money foolishly, but Harry gives all he has-- a sixpence. Suddenly, the bull gets loose, charges, Tommy falls trying to escape; his destruction appears certain when Harry seizes a prong and goes for the bull, wounding him in a flank. The bull leaves Tommy and would have killed Harry had not the grateful Negro attacked the bull with a stick. With much skill he finally gets the bull under control (295-96). The Black later tells his own story (444-45), the telling of which gives Day a chance for a few pointed remarks, such as: "Is a black horse thought to be inferior to a white one, in speed, or strength, or courage? Is a white cow thought to give more milk, or a white dog to have a more acute sense of smell in pursuing game?" (445) In The History of Little Jack, which is discussed in some detail at the end of the comments on Sandford and Merton, Day speaks of the treatment of a typical black by the whites: "[the white men] make him work hard with very little victuals, and knock him on the head if he attempted to run away."18

Although Day was more concerned with inequalities

among men, both Day and Rousseau felt their pupils should
be content with their own station in life. Harry tells Tommy: "A man must bear patiently whatever is his lot in this
world" (81). Both writers prepare their pupils for a change
in station with Day, as mentioned earlier, going to extremes
on the subject.

Day, then, was influenced in numerous ways by Rousseau, sometimes disagreeing, sometimes carrying to extremes a fundamental principle of Rousseau. This influence
is apparent also in Day's other book for children, The History of Little Jack, although not in the same degree or in
the same number of subjects, for Little Jack is a much
shorter work.

The History of Little Jack

Published first in 1788, as a part of The Children's
Miscellany, The History of Little Jack is seemingly an advance over Sandford and Merton in having a consistent and
well-formed plot. It charmed Richard Edgeworth, who found
fault only with the nanny goat.[19]

Day would not give up his nanny goat; he felt it was
an appropriate touch and a necessary part of the story, the
moral of which he states at the end: "It is of very little
consequence how a man comes into the world, provided he
behaves well and discharges his duty when he is in it."[20]
The purpose of the whole collection of stories in The Children's Miscellany was similar to that of this story--to improve knowledge and to inspire virtue.[21]

An old and lame ex-soldier finds little Jack after his
parents have deserted him. The old man takes Jack in and
relies upon God to provide for the little boy. The provision
is found in the form of a nanny goat who, as she has just
lost her own kid, is pleased to have little Jack to nurse.
There could hardly be a more humble beginning (413-14).
Jack grows up close to nature as Rousseau advocated. He
is unbound and unfettered by any swaddling clothes (414). On
one occasion when a wealthy lady gives him money to buy
some shoes, he finds, after trying to walk in a pair, that he
cannot stand to wear them (417). Rousseau believed a child
could go barefoot summer and winter.

Little Jack, through necessity and not through choice,

is educated along the lines Rousseau advocated. He learns
practical things, helping his adopted father, whom he calls
"Daddy," in the garden and doing the cooking. He gets lots
of exercise, playing with the goat, "Mamma," on the moors.
He knows nothing of lies, selfishness, and bad habits. His
daddy teaches him to write and read (415-16), however, at a
much earlier age than Rousseau would permit.

Like Tommy and unlike Emile, Jack acquires sensibility at an early age. He is kind and gentle and does everything he can for both his adopted parents, but both die in
spite of his efforts to help them. Jack is forced to go out
into the world at age twelve and make his own living (418).
He does so with some trials and tribulations, but in the end
he succeeds and is a very successful businessman in England.
He has the necessary ability, for he is self-reliant, eager to
learn every new trade, sensible, unafraid of hard work. His
only drawback is a pride in his humble origins. Whenever
his story gets out, people laugh at his mamma, a nanny goat.
Thus provoked, Jack will fight anyone, for he will not allow
laughter at his mamma.

Jack is one of the few characters in the story and the
only fully drawn one. A few of the others, however, are
worth mentioning. Daddy dies fairly quickly in the story, but
from what little is known of him, he does not seem to be of Rous-
seauistic origins. He is a poor lame old man, an ex-soldier,
who has a strong belief in God. He does not hesitate to try
to instruct Jack in morals and religion. He teaches by
words rather than examples. The following bit of dialogue
will show the kind of moral lesson which Rousseau opposed;
Daddy says to Jack: "'Never tell an untruth, Jack,' said he,
'even though you were to be flayed alive; a soldier never
lies.' Jack held up his head, marched across the floor, and
promised his daddy that he would always tell the truth, like
a soldier" (415).

Two other characters of interest appear in the story.
One is Master Willets, the little gentleman at whose house
Jack has the job of caring for the horses. Master Willets
is a good-natured boy, and he and Jack soon become friends.
Day describes Jack at this time as not only kind and good to
animals, but also "sober, temperate, hardy, active, and in-
genious, and [he] despised a lie as much as any of his bet-
ters" (425). Both Jack and the younger boy learn something
of accounts, writing, and geography from a thrice-weekly
visiting tutor (425). From the brief mention and short de-

scription of Master Willets, it would seem that he is in the
tradition of Emile, because of the manner of his education;
and for once Day has permitted a little gentleman to be good-
natured without having to be taught to be so through many
painful lessons.

The other interesting character in the story is a little
gentleman who, educated in France and accustomed to the
genteel life of London, comes to visit Master Willets. Day
condemns the youth in a single sentence: "His dress, too,
was a little particular, as well as his manners; for he spent
half his time in adjusting his head, wore a large black bag
tied to his hair behind, and would sometimes strut about for
half an hour together with his hat under his arm, and a little
sword by his side" (426). If Day felt a strong enough distaste
for fine clothes as to make the climax of Sandford and Merton occur when Tommy removes his finery and changes his
clothes to plain, simple ones, then it is obvious that Day has
little liking for this unnamed little gentleman. He is, as the
discussion of plot will show, essential to the action however.
He appears to have a prototype in some of the gentlemen of
Sandford and Merton, such as Master Mash, but I see no
prototype in Emile.

Rousseau's influence on plot seems almost nonexistent.
There is one incident, however, that shows both Day's and
Rousseau's love of Robinson Crusoe. The incident begins
with a remark made by the fancily-dressed gentleman; the
remark mortifies Jack. On the same day Jack chances upon
a showman with a monkey. The monkey charms Jack, so he
buys him, takes him home, and dresses him like the fancily-
dressed gentleman. When the latter catches a glimpse of the
former, he becomes enraged and runs the little monkey
through with his sword. Jack fights, and the young gentleman gets his clothes dirtied and his appearance spoiled.[22]
Jack refuses to apologize and thus loses his job (426-28).
He decides to become a soldier, as his adopted daddy was;
he sets sail for India. The ship stops at Cormo Island, off
the Coast of Africa where in search of game, Jack gets lost.
He soon realizes the ship has left without him. He adjusts
in the manner of Robinson Crusoe, an adjustment which Rousseau would have praised, and before long, Jack sights another ship which picks him up (429-32). Day finally has
achieved his ambition; he has gotten one of his characters to
that desert island that he has been preparing all of them for.

There does not appear to be any other example of

Rousseau's effect on plot other than the learning of various
trades which Rousseau advocated and which Jack is quick to
do. He learns farriery, carpentry, and saddlery. He also
learns the art of the blacksmith. Because of his knowledge
of farriery, he becomes a favorite of the Khan of the Tartars, with whom he is left as a hostage, by curing the favorite horse of the Khan (434).

After Jack's release from the Tartars, he returns to
England, where he becomes a successful businessman, who
never forgets the poor; thus ends the story. It has a few
new ideas, but on the whole, Day repeats his themes from
<u>Sandford and Merton</u>, many of which merely echoed Rousseau.
Again there is the idea of bodily development as well as
mental and moral development. Little Jack is plainly in the
tradition of Emile except for the fact that he was probably
not born a gentleman; as a foundling, no one can be sure of
his birthright. Yet he is reared and conducts himself in the
manner of an Emile reduced to straits of poverty.

In this novel, Day has Jack actually travel to faraway
lands instead of having a Mr. Barlow read about those places.
Rousseau advocated travel to round out an education, although
Emile's travels were considerably different from Jack's.
Day may have included the travels as a result of Emile's, or
he may have included them because he knew how children
love stories of faraway places, or perhaps he had both in
mind when he wrote.

Day in this second work relied upon Rousseau more
for character and for underlying principles of education than
he did for plot. Nevertheless, when both of Day's works are
considered together, the debt to Rousseau is truly of major consequence; for without a knowledge of <u>Emile</u>, they might never
have taken their place in the history of children's literature.

Notes

1.   "Preface," to <u>Sandford and Merton</u>, as cited by George
        Warren Gignilliat, Jr., <u>The Author of Sandford and
        Merton</u> (New York: Columbia University Press,
        1932), p. 263.

2.   Percival Horace Muir, <u>English Children's Books, 1600-
        1900</u> (New York: Praeger, 1954), p. 89, claims it
        was to be included in <u>Practical Education.</u> That is

obviously incorrect since Practical Education is not
composed of short stories, but rather of the authors'
philosophy of education.

3.	For a description of the reception of Sandford and Mer-
ton, see Gignilliat, p. 297-99. That author also includes a summary of the novel, p. 264-92, and a
survey of the editions and popularity of the novel,
p. 337-49. The influence of this novel upon later
writers is described in Gillian Elise Avery, Nineteenth Century Children: Heroes and Heroines in
English Children's Stories, 1780-1900 (London:
Hodder and Stoughton, 1965, p. 19-20.

4.	Gignilliat, p. 264.

5.	F. J. Harvey Darton, Children's Books in England:
Five Centuries of Social Life (Cambridge at the University Press, 1932), p. 146. Gignilliat also points
this out, p. 45.

6.	Gignilliat, p. 57.

7.	Ibid., p. 65.

8.	Ibid., p. 244-45.

9.	Thomas Day, The History of Sandford and Merton (rev.
Cecil Hartley; London: G. Routledge and Co.,
1858), p. 253-54. All future references in this
work will be indicated by the page numbers in parentheses in the body of the text.

10.	Interestingly enough, he makes no distinction between
the dialogue of the rich and that of the poor as
Muir, p. 93, points out.

11.	Gignilliat, p. 293. He also points out that Day re-
wards virtue unlike Rousseau who finds virtue a reward in itself.

12.	Gignilliat, p. 287, does mention the similarity between
Chares' philosophy and that of the Savoyard Vicar.

13.	Florence Valentine Barry, A Century of Children's
Books (New York: George H. Doran Co., 1923),
p. 112; and Gignilliat, p. 276, note this point also.

14. Gignilliat, p. 254.

15. Ibid., p. 293.

16. Ibid., p. 283. The speech of Sophron is on p. 323 of the edition of Sandford and Merton used here.

17. Ibid., p. 276.

18. Thomas Day, The History of Little Jack, in A Storehouse of Stories, ed. Charlotte M. Yonge (1st series; London: Macmillan, 1872), p. 431. This story also appears in Old-Fashioned Tales, selected by E. V. Lucas (London: Wells, Gardner, Darton and Co., 1905).

19. Gignilliat, p. 306-307.

20. Day, p. 431. All future references to this work will be indicated by the page numbers in parentheses in the body of the text.

21. Gignilliat, p. 300, quotes the "Preface" to the original edition.

22. Gignilliat, p. 96, claims this episode is a satire on Day's own attempt to learn the social graces.

Chapter IV

Maria Edgeworth

Thomas Day and Richard Edgeworth were very good friends who had similar beliefs about the education of children. Maria was the second of Edgeworth's many children. She submitted to him virtually all her writings, which he either approved or disapproved, and she always followed his advice. Since his stamp is upon all her writings, a brief consideration of his life and his beliefs about education and children will be made.

Richard Edgeworth came from a wealthy family of Edgeworthstown, Ireland. Reared in the overprotective manner so popular in his day, Edgeworth was always bundled up and never allowed to go without a hat; also he had to take medicines every spring and autumn as a preventative for worms.[1] In general, he did not look with favor upon the way in which his family reared him, and as a consequence he resolved to bring up his children in a somewhat different manner. His first son and oldest child he named Richard and called Dick; this is the boy mentioned in the chapter on Thomas Day who was reared in the tradition of Emile and who, when brought to meet Rousseau, failed to impress him favorably. As was mentioned previously (Chapter III), Rousseau met young Dick in Paris, accompanied by his father and Thomas Day. The boy and Rousseau went for a walk together; the result was that Rousseau found the boy knowledgeable and able, but prejudiced in favor of the English. It seems that Dick had praised an English horse and carriage that had passed. Rousseau found this prejudice a very serious fault and predicted that the boy would be governed by his companions later in life.[2]

The boy started out well enough. At eight years old, he was healthy, vivacious, and brave. He was good-natured, generous, and extremely independent. As a school boy, he was, however, somewhat unruly. He became a sailor and ultimately moved to America and settled in the Carolinas.

Needless to say, this was not what Mr. Edgeworth had
planned for his eldest son. At one point he decided to dis-
inherit the boy, but Day intervened. Day suggested the boy
be allowed his inheritance if he would return to Ireland.
Edgeworth was not to be persuaded. He did, however, leave
the boy some 300 pounds if he should return.[3] Thus this experiment of rearing the boy according to the principles set
forth in Emile ended unsatisfactorily, just as Day's experiment with the two girls did.

It is not surprising that the two experiments following
Rousseau's teaching failed. Rousseau's contribution to education was not so much in the propagation of his own somewhat
extreme ideas, but in causing a general reevaluation of earlier educational methods, methods which were apparently lacking. The writings of Day and Edgeworth, as well as Maria's,
helped to popularize Rousseau's teachings. Maria knew Day
and visited him when she was only fourteen and suffering
from extremely poor eyesight. Day treated her with tarwater
and exposed her to good books. In spite of this, Maria's
eyes were cured, and she learned to love and respect her
father's friend.[4] She never met Rousseau himself, but there
can be no doubt that she knew his writings well from Day,
her father, and even her brother Dick. She also knew of
Rousseau indirectly from her first literary work which was a
translation of Madame de Genlis' Adèle et Théodore. Madame
de Genlis was a French disciple of Rousseau.

That Richard and Maria wrote their monumental work,
Practical Education, while under the influence of Rousseau,
seems clear. This work, written earlier but not published
until 1797, contains many of the ideas which appear in The
Parent's Assistant (originally called Parent's Friend), Moral
Tales, and Early Lessons. The Edgeworths had plenty of
time to evaluate and revise the ideas as they desired: for by
1797, Mr. Edgeworth had had three wives and fifteen or sixteen children.[5] Maria was thirty years old and had been,
since she was fifteen, in charge of some of the younger children, a duty which she seems to have thoroughly enjoyed.
Obviously, these two had a good bit of experience in the practical application of educational theory.

Briefly, the main points of agreement with Rousseau
in Practical Education are on the attitude toward servants being helpful but not slaves,[6] on the idea that words without
knowledge and understanding of them are useless (I, 97), on
the idea of the tutor listening as well as speaking to his pupil

(I, 151), on the way Rousseau develops the senses and judgment of the child (III, 195). They disagreed about Rousseau's point that children are naturally gluttons (I, 197), about the cunning which Rousseau suggests women have (I, 258), about Rousseau's idea that the child should not know that in doing his elder's will, he is being obedient (I, 274), about Emile's tutor teaching truth by falsehood (I, 296), and in the attitude toward habit. Emile is to have no habits; but the Edgeworths felt that habit was necessary: every trivial occasion should not require the use of reason (III, 265).

In general there are two main concepts which govern all the writings of the Edgeworths. The first--the idea of utility or usefulness--definitely came from Rousseau. The second--the teaching of morals without any mention of religion--may have come from Rousseau. It was certainly an unusual practice for its time, and Rousseau would have condoned it. It is possible, however, that the Edgeworths did not mention religion because they were Protestants in Catholic Ireland. Edgeworth, in the words of Isabel Clarke, pitied rather than disliked Catholics. Maria, continues Isabel Clarke, had little knowledge of, and no sympathy for, Catholicism, but because she wrote for both Catholic and Protestant children, she had to inculcate the moral lessons without arousing prejudice.[7] Whether following in the path of Rousseau or using a practical approach in regard to the market for her books, Maria makes no mention of religion in her works, although she certainly does teach morals as such a book as Early Lessons shows.

Early Lessons

The final version of Early Lessons falls well beyond the period covered in this paper. Certain parts of it, however, were definitely written prior to 1800. The first part written was Harry and Lucy, the joint effort of Richard Edgeworth and his second (and by his own admission, favorite) wife, Honora Sneyd. It was the work which Edgeworth designed to follow Mrs. Barbauld's Lessons for Children. It was for Harry and Lucy that Day wrote Sandford and Merton, intending to include it as a short story. Harry and Lucy definitely shows the influence of Rousseau. Maria's part in it does not come until later. She added to Harry and Lucy, writing off and on between 1814 and 1825.

In 1801, the first edition of Maria's Early Lessons

appeared. In 1816, Maria continued it. In the 1825 American edition of Maria's works,[8] the Harry-Lucy stories, both
Richard's and Maria's, appear with Maria's creations--the
beloved Rosamond, the too-good Frank,[9] and others--all under the title Early Lessons, which comprises almost three
volumes of the thirteen-volume series of her works.[10] In
addition to the stories by Richard and Honora Sneyd, there is
a group which Maria wrote prior to 1800. This date is ver-
ifiable because they originally appeared in The Parent's Assistant (1796), and Maria transferred them to Early Lessons;
they are: "The Little Dog Trusty," "The Orange Man," and
"The Purple Jar."[11] Maria probably transferred these stories, according to Dobson, because they were written for a
much younger child[12] and The Parent's Assistant is primarily
for older children. I shall briefly discuss these three, one
of which introduces Maria's most well-known character Rosamond, to show what the other quite lengthy stories of Early
Lessons attempt to do.

       In "The Little Dog Trusty or the Liar and the Boy of
Truth,"[13] Maria contrasts two eight-year-old brothers; one
is Frank, the hero of many of Maria's tales; the other is
Robert, a coward who tells lies. While playing with Trusty,
the dog, the two boys accidentally knock over some milk.
Frank decides to run and tell his mother immediately, regardless of the punishment.[14] Robert begs him not to go
(IX, 23). A few minutes later Robert sees his mother and
knows she has not yet seen Frank. He tells his mother that
Trusty spilled the milk. His mother decides to beat Trusty;
Frank's arrival with the true story saves Trusty from a beating (IX, 24). The boys' father arrives, beats Robert with
the switch intended for Trusty, and tells both boys they can
have no milk for supper. This episode is a good one to demonstrate Rousseau's principle of punishment fitting the crime;
however, Maria goes further than Rousseau would have
wished. She rewards Frank for his honesty and gives him
Trusty for his own. Trusty's name is changed to Frank.
If anyone wishes to know why the dog's name is changed, he
is to be told the story of the liar and the truthful boy
(IX, 25).

       "The Orange Man: or, The Honest Boy and the Thief"
is so similar that it will be mentioned only briefly. The
good boy receives a reward of some oranges which he pro-
tected from the little thief who tried to steal them (IX, 28).
This time, however, in opposition to Rousseau's preference
for unstated moral, Maria states several maxims at the end:

"People must be honest before they can be generous"; "it is
never worth while to do wrong" (IX, 29).

The third story transferred to Early Lessons was "The
Purple Jar," Maria's most famous story in which Rosamond,
her best-known character, appears. Every serious critic of
Miss Edgeworth's writings has discussed this story. To
summarize it in a sentence or two is not to do it justice.
It is a good example of Rousseau's doctrine of usefulness.
As was mentioned earlier, Mr. Edgeworth believed in the
doctrine of usefulness also, only he demanded usefulness from
girls, as well as from boys. Rousseau felt girls should concern themselves with the effect of their actions, not the usefulness of them. Rosamond, who at least one critic believes
to be Maria herself,[15] has the choice of a purple jar, in
which she hopes to put flowers, or a new pair of shoes, her
present ones having a hole in the bottom. Rosamond decides
in favor of the jar; her punishment suits her so-called crime.
The purple in the jar turns out to be a chemical which when
thrown out makes the jar just like any other (IX, 150); the
shoes get so bad that Rosamond cannot walk without pain;
she may not go with her father on one occasion when she
wants to because she walks slip-shod (IX, 151). Rosamond
learns by experience, the method Rousseau advocated. Thus
Early Lessons shows the influence of a few major ideas of
Rousseau.

The Parent's Assistant

The Parent's Assistant, however, shows the influence
of Rousseau in a number of ways. The purpose, as stated
in the "Preface" written by Mr. Edgeworth, is not to make
the child wise beyond his years, but to teach him those
things which all classes have in common: justice, truth, and
humanity (X, vi). He says that the useful is more important
than the artistic, hence Maria does not include any poetical
allusions (X, vii). Edgeworth next discusses the problem of
reward in several stories, then states that in his daughter's
stories, she has attempted "to provide antidotes against ill-
humor, the epidemic rage for dissipation, and the fatal pro-
pensity to admire and imitate whatever the fashion of the
moment may distinguish" (X, viii). These statements are all
in keeping with Rousseau's ideas, but Edgeworth's next statement directly contradicts the principle of negative education
where children are to be kept from all vice: "But in real
life [children] must see vice, and it is best that they should

be early shocked with the representation of what they are to
avoid" (X, viii). In order to shock them, it is necessary to
make the stories somewhat dramatic.[16]

Edgeworth concludes the "Preface" by stating that clut-
tering up the child's mind with fairies and giants and fantas-
tic visions only wastes time and prevents useful knowledge
from entering the child's mind (X, viii). What he is doing
is refuting Dr. Johnson's argument in favor of children's
imaginations being cultivated. Rousseau would obviously have
opposed Dr. Johnson also.

The characters in The Parent's Assistant are the most
realistic and interesting covered thus far in this study except perhaps for some of those in Early Lessons. One critic
has divided Maria's characters into types of which there are
variations: "the wise sister and playful brother; the well-
informed brother with a thoughtless sister; the wise or
thoughtless one with a foolish or a prudential family."[17] This
classification is good, as far as it goes. In each case, there
is contrast between good and bad; and as another critic
points out, the children's behavior is not always predicta-
ble.[18] This critic also lists a few hateful and a few flawless characters.[19] The term hateful seems inappropriately
harsh because these children are just naughty, primarily because they have received the wrong kind of education; however, the naughty evoke no sympathy for themselves from the
reader. Included in the list of hateful characters are Barbara
Case in "Simple Susan" and Bell in "The Birthday Present."
The list of flawless characters consists of Laura in "The
Birthday Present" and Ben in "Waste Not, Want Not."[20]
"Simple Susan" and "The Birthday Present" are typical and as
good as any to use in order to see the extent of Rousseau's
influence. Unfortunately, there are too many stories in The
Parent's Assistant to discuss each one.

In "Simple Susan," Susan Price, a farmer's twelve-
year-old daughter, is in contrast to Barbara Case, a lawyer's
daughter. It is interesting that Barbara's father is a bad
man; it is as if to say Barbara inherited her badness, or at
least had not the proper education nor proper example from
her parent. She is, as Lucas points out, like the bad boy
in "The Ill-Natured Little Boy" in Sandford and Merton whose
father is also bad.[21] Susan is sweet, kind, and consequently
popular. Barbara has no friends. Susan is industrious--she
bakes bread (X, 21), knows accounts (X, 31), and cares for
her brothers (X, 31). She is, to use Maria's word, indefati-

Maria Edgeworth 85

gable in all ways Rousseau's Sophie was.

Susan's father disagrees with Attorney Case about a
piece of land with the result that Mr. Case claims Mr.
Price must pay off his lease at once. Since he must pay off
the lease, Mr. Price will have to enter the militia because
he can no longer pay for a substitute. Then Mr. Case, an
example of the corrupt society that Rousseau feared, finds a
flaw in the lease, and, consequently, has the Prices at his
mercy. In an effort to please a highborn gentleman's taste
for lamb, Mr. Case proposes to Susan that she give up her
pet lamb for a week's extension of the date on which her
father must leave (X, 29). Poor Susan hardly hesitates, although it breaks her heart to give up her beloved lamb,
Daisy. The attorney's plan does not work, for the butcher
believes it is a sin to kill a pet lamb and sends another lamb
in Daisy's place (X, 40). Susan does not know this and believes her Daisy is gone forever. Here is an act of true
generosity; Susan has no idea that she will receive a reward.
She does, for the highborn gentleman in the neighborhood, Sir
Arthur, sees to the straightening out of the lease so Mr.
Price does not have to enter the militia, Susan gets her lamb
back, and the piece of disputed land is made into a play-
green for the children. Attorney Case is in disgrace for trying to swindle Mr. Price and for trying to have Susan's lamb
killed as a present for Sir Arthur. Although this brief summary does not show how hateful Barbara is, perhaps this
quality in her is obvious from the fact that she keeps Susan's
little hen which accidentally entered the Cases' property.
Susan's friends finally buy the hen back from Barbara. It is
Barbara's suggestion that her father can find no fatter lamb
than Susan's Daisy. Barbara's punishment is only embarrass-
ment and, of course, loneliness, because she has no friends.
Although Susan's reward fits her virtuous acts, Barbara's
punishment does not fit her evil ways. Here, both rewards
and punishments are not strictly following Rousseau's doctrine.

It is the type of education from good parents that Susan has, along with the principle of usefulness, that makes
"Simple Susan" follow the tradition of Rousseau. "The Birthday Present," another Rosamond story, puts the doctrine of
usefulness first. Rosamond spends her money and her time
in making a basket for her cousin Bell's birthday. As the
basket is very fancy and delicate, its usefulness is exceeding-
ly limited (X, 149). Bell is the hateful character because
she is so completely spoiled. Maria describes Bell: "Everyone in the house tried to please her, and they succeeded so

well, that between breakfast and dinner she had only six fits
of crying" (X, 151). Bell is as different from Rousseau's
Sophie as anyone can be. Edgeworth.points out in the "Preface" that Bell is the product of education by a bad servant
(X, vii); Rousseau would agree about not letting just anyone
educate a child. Bell's personality only serves to make the
good girl even more attractive. The good girl in the story
is Laura, who is as good as Bell is bad and as Rosamond is
foolish.

Laura does not waste her money foolishly as Rosamond
does. When Laura and Rosamond witness a footman's destroying a little girl's pillow which she is weaving (X, 148),
Rosamond feels sorry for the little girl, but Laura gives the
little girl enough money to buy new materials. Laura is truly generous; whereas Rosamond is foolish, even though Rosamond thinks she is doing the right thing. Once again Rosamond seems harshly treated, but she is again learning by
experience, which is the best teacher, according to Rousseau.

Before closing the discussion of the characters of "The
Birthday Present," I must comment on the tutor. In this
story, as in many of Maria's stories, the parents serve, as
Rousseau wished, as tutors for their children. There is no
doubt that Rosamond will turn out to be an admirable young
lady, and her tutors--her mother and her father--certainly
are in the tradition of Rousseau. They are practically without mercy when it comes to teaching the child a lesson.
Just as Rousseau's tutor would have Emile believe he was
really lost in the forest, Rosamond's mother lets her buy the
purple jar and her father rebukes her for spending her time
and money on a present for her cousin Bell's birthday. He
says:

> To make a present of a thing that you know can be
> of no use [the basket she made is too delicate], to
> a person you neither love nor esteem, because it
> is her birth-day, and because every body [sic]
> gives her something, and because she expects some-
> thing, and because your godmother says she likes
> that people should be generous, seems to me my
> dear Rosamond, to be, since I must say it, rather
> more like folly than generosity. (X, 150)

It is the fact that Rosamond tried to be unselfish and yet still
met with parental disapproval that makes Rosamond such a
human and sympathetic character.

The plots of these two stories are simple and straight-
forward, growing in each case out of a single incident: the
argument between Mr. Price and Mr. Case and the prepara-
tions for Bell's birthday. Maria carefully rewards each good
child. I have mentioned Susan Price's reward; Laura, Rosamond's sister, gets her reward when the little girl to whom
she gave money for a new pillow arrives at Bell's house to
delivery some lace she has made for Bell's dress. She recognizes Laura and reveals to all present what a generous
girl Laura is; thus she receives praise from all.

Although these two stories do not have surprise endings, there are others in The Parent's Assistant which do,
such as "Old Poz," "Eton Montem," and "The Bracelets." One
critic calls Maria a pioneer of plot in children's books and
claims, and rightly so, that there is often a surprise in the
way Maria solves the puzzle of each story. [22] Rousseau
would not oppose surprises, for he often used tricks to cap-
ture Emile's attention.

The subjects treated by Maria are limited to ones
from which moral lessons are obvious; that is, there is no
discussion of the manufacture of paper, for example, as in
Evenings at Home for the purpose of learning how paper is
made. [23] One of Maria's favorite topics is benevolence towards the poor as in "Waste Not, Want Not." Another theme
is seen by the title of "Forgive and Forget." There are many
more lessons on the subjects of generosity, honesty, good-
naturedness, industry, self-reliance, and others. Maria differs from Rousseau in these teachings in that she often states
the moral, even stating it herself instead of allowing a character to do so, that she uses the same lessons for boys as
for girls, and that she gives examples of bad children and
vices which are in opposition to Rousseau's idea of negative
education. She follows Rousseau in the type of subject
treated, in learning by experience, and in giving the child the
desire to learn. In her thesis Miss Stevens points out many
of these similarities, and she also mentions Maria's following
Rousseau in developing the ability to reason rather than ac-
cumulating knowledge, and Maria's not following Rousseau in
showing that excellence results from effort and interest;
whereas Rousseau claims interest is enough as a basis for
learning. [24]

Moral Tales

Many of the same conclusions hold true for Moral Tales (1800), a work written for older children in which Maria, in the words of one critic, "mocked rather than condemned, and in so doing introduced an entirely new element to the juvenile tale--humour."[25] Mr. Edgeworth states the purpose in the "Preface": "to provide for young people, of a more advanced age, a few Tales, that shall neither dissipate the attention, nor inflame the imagination" (IX, 61). He claims that Maria wrote these stories expressly to illustrate opinions set forth in Practical Education (IX, 62). Here again, as in Maria's The Parent's Assistant, Edgeworth points out the moral or purpose of most of the stories in the collection. The two stories chosen for discussion are "Forester," which one critic says is without doubt the best story in Moral Tales, and "The Good French Governess," which the same critic calls a good story.[26]

Both "Forester" and "The Good Governess" show the impact of Rousseau's teaching more than does Early Lessons, which was written for younger children. "Forester" is the story of a young English boy, the son of a gentleman, who is brave, generous, and extremely independent. He knows little of polite society; the inequality between the rich and the poor shocks him (IX, 63). When he is nineteen, his father dies; and he goes to live with Dr. Campbell of Edinburgh, a learned and kindly man, with a son of his own just a few years older than Forester (IX, 64). Henry Campbell is in contrast to Forester in the story. He is a gentleman at ease in society; whereas Forester is ill at ease in dining, in conversing with ladies, and in other customs of polite society. Newby makes the interesting remark, and not an unfounded one, that Forester is really Richard Edgeworth. His reasons are as follows:

> [Forester] refuses to dress according to his station in life, he despises dancing and girls, and runs away from his kind guardian to take a job as a gardener. Henry, the guardian's son, is on the other hand a complete Edgeworth boy. He never acts precipitately and bears himself like a man of forty. Furthermore he has the world of science at his fingertips. He is able to save the life of a friend's canary because he has read Falconer's treatise on poisons. The climax of the story is reached when Forester is falsely accused of stealing a banknote

and Henry is able to establish his innocence by
keen observation, close reasoning and a knowledge
of the effects of vitrolic acid.[27]

Forester admits he has been foolish and gives in to Henry's
way of life. Newby says of the end of the story: "The story
gives some measure of the distance that Mr. Edgeworth had
travelled since his early enthusiasm for Rousseau. It is the
story of civilisation triumphant."[28]

It is true, as Newby points out, that Forester admits
his mistake in the end; yet Forester is the protagonist and a
thoroughly admirable young man who is unafraid of hard work
and is scrupulously honest. His kindness to animals twice
gets him into trouble; on the second occasion, he interferes
when he sees little dancing dogs exhausted and in need of
rest. He does what Rousseau said Emile should do--prevent
cruelty; but he gets into a fight in doing it (IX, 112). He is
impetuous; this characteristic also gets him into trouble with
the dancing master, for he listens to only one side of a tale
and not the other (IX, 67). Later he gets into trouble with
the teacher of a little girl whom he is trying to help (IX, 74).
Because of his imprudence, the little girl gets beaten. Yet
he does as Rousseau suggested; he gives of himself, not just
of his money. He has to learn, however, the proper way to
give of himself. He impetuously decides to earn his own
living--Rousseau felt every boy should be capable of doing so
and Day felt the boy should use that capability.

Forester gradually makes the transformation from a
character in the tradition of Emile or Day, who is truly a
misfit in society, into the knowledgeable, effective, helpful
type in the tradition of Edgeworth. Forester even has certain characteristics of Rosamond, who, as mentioned earlier,
may have been Maria herself. Both are often foolish, but it
is that quality that makes them lovable and human. Henry
is like Laura, Rosamond's sister, always good, always doing
the proper thing, less human, but not as goody-goody as
Frank in Early Lessons.

Both Henry and Dr. Campbell serve as tutors for Forester, but Henry is more often on the scene. Henry is always using his head or his hands (IX, 66), a fact which is in
keeping with the doctrine of usefulness. Henry's love of science is in keeping with Edgeworth's own love of it. Rousseau
was less interested in chemistry than in botany, but both believed in the importance of the child's learning something of

the sciences. It is significant that this entire discussion has
mentioned Mr. Edgeworth and not Maria who actually wrote
the story; but she always wrote to please her father, and she
held him in such esteem that she actually believed as he did.
Thus, Edgeworth's ideas are synonymous with Maria's.

Dr. Campbell is one of the main spokesmen for Maria.
He agrees with Maria and Rousseau that Forester should
learn by experience (IX, 95). He is one of the characters
who exemplifies in his teaching what the critic had in mind
when she said that Maria introduced humor as a way of
teaching.[29] Dr. Campbell uses "playful raillery" and "well-
timed reasoning" in his teaching (IX, 65). On one occasion
he thought to himself: "Folly . . . could be as effectively
corrected by the tickling of a feather, as by the lash of the
satirist" (IX, 86). He puts this philosophy into action immediately in order to settle a quarrel between two ladies as
to who is to have precedency on the dance floor. Campbell
calmly remarks that he is sure that the younger one will give
the pleasure to the older. The result is as expected, and
finally the ladies draw lots (IX, 86). Although Campbell
speaks for Maria, he is not truly in the tradition of Rousseau's tutor, for he is too human and unwilling to resort to
deceit in any form.

In plot, Maria follows some ideas of Rousseau, but
she is not a slave to them. She has examples of punishment
befitting the crime as, for example, when Forester learns
the little girl whom he tried to help was beaten because he
had gone about trying to aid her in an impulsive, rash manner (IX, 129-30).[30] Maria has Forester admit after this
episode that he is "a useless being." This is serious con-
demnation from the point of view of the Edgeworths, Rousseau, and other followers of the doctrine of usefulness.

Rousseau's concepts govern plot to the extent that
when Forester feels he can no longer face the life of polite
society, he seeks the simple life of a gardener because he
claims he is not fit to live with idle gentlemen and ladies--
he wants to be useful (IX, 92). Just as Rousseau felt civili-
zation, especially in cities, corrupts, so Forester learns
that people can be corrupt in any walk of life, in the country
or city. The gardener's daughter is vain, ugly, and cross.
The gardener's son is lazy and without ambition; he spends
much time at goff (sic). The gardener is uneducated and refuses to listen to Forester's scheme for making the cherry
trees bear twice as many cherries. Forester becomes dis-

gusted and returns to the city; he still intends, however, to
earn his own way. It is of interest that Forester chooses
agriculture, an occupation greatly admired by Rousseau and
Day for its usefulness, and then rejects it. This action
seems to show rejection of Rousseau's theory; yet in another
way, it illustrates another principle of Rousseau: one should
seek and be content with his station in life. Forester knows
too much about cherry trees; consequently, he is not content
to follow his uneducated master's advice about the trees.
Thus Forester learns something by experience, the method
of teaching that Rousseau advocated.

The ideas of Rousseau, or a rejection of them, are
also obvious in the themes and subjects treated by Maria.
Rousseau believed in independence. Forester does also, for
he says "my mind to me a kingdom is." A little later, however, Maria comments that separated from other people, "his
mind, however enlarged would afford him but a dreary kingdom" (IX, 110). Also somewhat contradictory to Rousseau's
emphasis on exercise is Henry's thought that being able to
walk a number of miles without being tired is not especially
admirable. Forester on this occasion has just claimed that
it was and that gentlemen were effeminate because they could
not. Henry claims it is not the highest perfection of human
nature (IX, 79). It should not be said that the Edgeworths
opposed aiding physical fitness by walking, but the above con-
versation seems to consider physical fitness to be of less
importance than Rousseau would consider it to be.

In keeping with Rousseau's feeling that all habits are undesirable, the Edgeworths gave Forester the undesirable habit of
twirling things. Rousseau, of course, did not want Emile to
have any habits, and the lack of perfection in this respect
leads Forester into trouble. He twirls a key which falls to
the bottom of a vat in a brewery. A young employee de-
scends to get the key, and the bad air renders him uncon-
scious. Forester, impulsive and anxious to right the situation which he has caused, hurries down the ladder and also
falls insensible. Henry, on the other hand, has that presence of mind that Aikin tried to teach to his readers, and he
throws water down the vat to expel the bad air (IX, 80-81).
The two are saved thanks to Henry's quick thinking. Any
kind of habit is bad says Rousseau, but Maria claims a bad
habit can be deadly.

Maria is in agreement with Rousseau on several other
points as well. She has young Forester avidly read a book

about "the history of a man, who had been cast away some
hundred years ago upon a desert island" (IX, 77). It is quite
likely that the title of this book, although not mentioned, is
none other than the first and foremost book in Emile's li-
brary--Robinson Crusoe. Forester liked the book because he
is similar to Crusoe; Maria describes him as "inclined to
prefer the life of Robinson Crusoe" (IX, 63).

Maria states a few morals explicitly in the story,
such as "Forester resolved, that, before he ever again attempted to do justice, he would, at least, hear both sides of
the question" (IX, 68). But, in general, the morals are implied from the lessons Forester learns; Rousseau felt the
unstated moral was best.

The same principle holds true for the maxims in "The
Good French Governess," in which the central character is
the governess rather than the children she teaches. She is
in keeping with the ideal governess that Rousseau described
in his letter to the Duke of Wurtemberg, dated November 16,
1763; that is, she is not too young nor too handsome; she is
a widow with none of her children near her; she is neither
flighty nor frivolous; she is gentle, calm, and intelligent,
but not brilliant. She loves the children under her care; she
knows what she is to teach and is confident of her success;
and finally, she has absolute authority over the children.[31]
The governess, Madame de Rosier, possesses all the qualities mentioned above. Later in the story, however, she discovers her long lost son, and at that point she gives up her
job as governess. She is as ideal a character as any Maria
created. She has complete charge of the four Harcourt children: Isabella, fourteen; Matilda, thirteen; Herbert, eight;
and Favoretta, six. Maria describes Madame de Rosier's
control over the children when she has Mrs. Harcourt state:
"Madame de Rosier and I are always of one mind about the
children" (IX, 323).

Because of the setting, which involves teaching every
day, this story shows more of the influence of Rousseau's
Emile than any other one by Maria discussed so far. There
are, after all, many more opportunities to show teaching
methods and lessons. Each child learns according to his individual bent as Rousseau advocated. Isabella has too much
confidence in her own ability, and her memory is too much
cultivated (IX, 298). Rousseau would not object to the first,
but he certainly would oppose the second. Matilda has too
little confidence and, consequently, puts out little effort to

learn (IX, 298). Here Miss Stevens' comment cited earlier
is applicable: for Rousseau, interest was enough for learning, but for Maria, interest plus effort were necessary.[32]

The third child, Herbert, refuses to learn to read, is
obstinate, and is bashful in, and adverse to, polite society
(IX, 299). The governess encourages his desire to read in
exactly the same manner as Emile's tutor did; in fact, Maria cites Rousseau in a footnote at the end of the episode
(IX, 312). Herbert is much younger than Emile, however,
when he learns to read. It is interesting that Herbert reads
from Mrs. Barbauld's "excellent little books" and from Evenings at Home, and has Sandford and Merton read to him (IX,
318). Herbert's obstinate quality is overcome by Madame de
Rosier's application of the theory of usefulness. She sees
to it that all the children get useful toys; in Herbert's case,
he receives a printing press, which is partially responsible
for his desire to read, and a packet of radish seeds. He
thus takes up the useful occupation of gardening (IX, 306-
307). Herbert becomes more independent through learning to
be useful and learning to read. He learns about the property
of others and what he can meddle with and what he cannot
(IX, 310-11). He thus learns many of the same lessons that
Emile learned, but at a much younger age.

Favoretta is too young to have many habits; yet she
could easily be called spoiled since she is the baby and receives much attention (IX, 298). Madame de Rosier deals
with each of the children's problems separately and, generally speaking, in the same way Rousseau would. For example,
she takes Herbert to see the various tradesmen and crafts-
men at work (IX, 311). She uses models and pictures whenever possible, according to Maria, "to enlarge his ideas of
visible objects" (IX, 311). She seems to fit Rousseau's concept of a governess in every way except for his idea that the
tutor or governess should be of the same sex as the pupil.
The tenet is adhered to in the cases of the three female children, of course, but not in the case of Herbert.

The two older girls, encouraged to do those things
which they do best, are not put in competition with one another. Rousseau felt the child should be in competition with
himself only. It turns out that Matilda, while not good at
memorizing like her sister, is very good with arithmetic.
The arithmetic lesson arises from an incident involving Herbert. Herbert shows his sister an ant crawling up a stick.
Madame de Rosier, fond of analogy and quick to inject a les-

son whenever feasible, tells Herbert and Matilda this problem:

> This snail was to crawl up a wall, twenty feet
> high; he crawled up five feet every day, and
> slipped back again four feet every night;--in how
> many days did he reach the top of the wall? (IX,
> 316)

Matilda quickly whispers the answer.[33] Matilda is closer to
Rousseau's ideal Sophie than Isabella is because of her modest manner.

It is with Isabella that Madame de Rosier appears to
part from Rousseau's ways. For example, Isabella receives
books of poetry to read to cultivate her imagination (IX, 316).
Rousseau felt poetry was to delight; and he said nothing
about the imagination. Isabella learns to be a more agree-
able conversationalist because she stops loading her mind
with historical and chronological facts. Maria philosophizes:
"When the memory is overloaded, the imagination, or the in-
ventive faculty, often remains inactive; wit, as well as invention, depends upon the quick combination of ideas" (IX,
317). Rousseau never aspired for Emile to become a wit;
thus Madame de Rosier's object with regard to Isabella seems
to differ from Rousseau's; but this appears to be one of the
few ways in which the characters differ, after being educated,
from Rousseau's ideal.

The plot, on the other hand, shows less evidence of
Rousseau's teaching. It is complex compared to the plots of
the stories in The Parent's Assistant or those in Early Lessons. Of course, Maria wrote Moral Tales for older children. This plot like the one in "Forester" has few surprises
and mysteries. There is one case of the punishment suiting
the crime: the maid who is jealous of Madame de Rosier,
entices the younger children to disobey; and she ultimately
loses her job because she does so. There is also the episode of Miss Fanshaw, an episode which is not necessary to
the plot, but which apparently was included for the purpose
of emphasizing Rousseau's point that education by a governess
or tutor is superior to education at school. Both Miss Fanshaw's actions in public and in private are thoroughly obnox-
ious. She has two sides to her character, both unappealing.
In condemning her, the reader condemns, as Rousseau did,
education at school.

There are several other examples of the effect of
Rousseau's ideas on the plot. One is that Madame de Rosier,
who fled from France during the reign of Robespierre--one
of the few references to current events in any of the books
discussed here--lost contact with her son and believes him to
be dead. In the course of the story, she discovers her son
and the two are reunited. A little box, which the son made
and which the Harcourt girls admire greatly, is the instrument
which eventually leads to his discovery. Henri, the son, is
able to support himself after escaping from jail in France,
by making and selling those little boxes. He is the perfect
example of the idea which Rousseau stated that a young man
should be able to support himself if such an emergency ever
arose. Henri de Rosier describes his early education: "Now
it was that I felt the advantage of being taught, when I was a
boy, the use of carpenters' tools, and some degree of me-
chanical dexterity" (IX, 358). Thus he became skillful at
carpentry, the same kind of skill that Rousseau wished Emile
to acquire.

After the reunion of mother and son, the son's patron-
ess, lady N---, sees to it that Madame de Rosier's property
in France is restored to her and her son. Mrs. Harcourt
thus takes over the education of her own children. Rousseau
felt the mother was the best tutor for her daughters, but in
this case, the mother had to learn a few things before she
was able to take over efficiently. These things she learned
from Madame de Rosier.

In this story the subjects treated by Maria which show
the influence of Rousseau are numerous. I have already
mentioned some in the discussions of plot and character. I
shall review here only those not previously treated. One subject is fashion. Miss Fanshaw remarks about the lack of
taste in people of other generations (IX, 348). She obviously
is one who changes with the times. Rousseau, of course,
unable to think as a woman, thought it ridiculous to change
with the fashions all the time if what one had was becoming.
Miss Fanshaw's mother, another unadmirable character, uses
this occasion to defend whalebone stays and long waists (IX,
348). Rousseau was specifically against any kind of clothing
for women which was tight or which distorted the figure.

Another subject, perhaps following Rousseau's lead, is
the lack of religious education. Maria states:

Mrs. Harcourt, . . . invested Madame de Rosier

> with full powers as the perceptress of her children,
> except as to their religious education . . . Madame
> de Rosier readily promised to abstain from all di-
> rect or indirect interference, in the religious in-
> struction of her pupils. (IX, 299-300).

Although she does not teach religion, Madame de Rosier has occasion to teach her pupils about generosity (IX,
349) and about presence of mind (IX, 337-38). Maria also
includes an example of Henri's following the advice given to
Emile to always ascertain the cause of any suffering (IX,
359). There is even an example of Rousseau's idea which
coincided with the Edgeworths' idea in Practical Education of
the importance of understanding every word one reads (IX,
332).

The idea of children being gluttonous if not properly
trained appears in a description of Herbert. Maria makes a
point about overeating and about generosity when she says:

> Herbert had, formerly, to use his own expression,
> been accused of being fond of eating, and so, per-
> haps he was; but since he had acquired other plea-
> sures, those of affection and employment, his love
> of eating had diminished so much, that he had eaten
> only one of his own radishes, because he felt more
> pleasure in distributing the rest to his mother and
> sisters. (IX, 326)

In spite of all these subjects which follow Rousseau's
thinking, there is one example which seems to contradict
Rousseau. Maria says of Madame de Rosier: "[She] never
made use of artifices upon any occasion to get rid of children" (IX, 339). Here she simply tells Herbert to leave the
room because she is going to talk about something which she
does not want him to hear. Rousseau may not have used
artifices to get rid of children, but he certainly used artifices.

Thus, Maria followed Rousseau's teachings more often
than not. She followed her father at all times of course, and
he became somewhat disenchanted with Rousseau, but retained
respect for many of the latter's educational ideas. Maria,
though certainly didactic, sometimes permits the story to be
as important as the moral. It is perhaps for this reason
that her works are the only ones considered here which have
been reprinted in the last twenty-five years. Almost every
critic of children's literature calls her the best storyteller of

her period. For example, Muir calls her the first who had a narrative gift,34 and Miss Meigs says: "In spite of Richard Edgeworth, in spite of Thomas Day, in spite even of Jean Jacques Rousseau, Maria was too great a writer to suffer herself to be led completely astray."35

Notes

1. Richard Lovell Edgeworth, Memoirs of Richard Lovell Edgeworth, Esq. (2 vols.; London: Hunter, 1810), I, 31, as cited by George Warren Gignilliat, Jr., The Author of Sandford and Merton (New York: Columbia University Press, 1932), p. 39.

2. Gignilliat, p. 95.

3. Isabel C. Clarke, Maria Edgeworth: Her Family and Friends (London: Hutchinson and Co., 1949?), p. 42, claims Dick did return to Ireland for the last time in 1795. By this time he was married; and by 1798, when he died, he was the father of three sons.

4. Mr. Edgeworth's respect for Day is seen by the fact that upon learning of Day's death resulting from being thrown by a horse, Edgeworth named his day-old son Thomas Day Edgeworth. The child like so many of those born to Edgeworth's second and third wives died very young, at three years to be exact.

5. The exact number is not known. For as complete a list as any I have seen of the children and wives of Edgeworth, see Clarke, page opposite "Foreword."

6. Maria and R. L. Edgeworth, Practical Education (3 vols.; 2nd ed.; London: J. Johnson, 1801), I, 195. All future references to this work will be indicated by the volume numbers and page numbers in parentheses in the body of the text.

7. Clarke, p. 106-107.

8. Maria Edgeworth, The Works of Maria Edgeworth (13 vols.; Boston: Samuel H. Parker, 1824-1826).

9. For criticism of these two characters, see, among others, Clarke, p. 42; F. J. Harvey Darton, Children's

Books in England: Five Centuries of Social Life
(Cambridge at the University Press, 1932), p. 143;
E. V. Lucas, "Introduction," to Old-Fashioned Tales,
selected by E. V. Lucas (London: Wells, Gardner,
Darton and Co. , 1905), p. viii, and Charlotte M.
Yonge, "Children's Literature of the Last Century,"
Living Age, CII (September 4, 1869), 614.

10. See vols. XI, XII, XIII.

11. M. Edgeworth, X, viii. For a complete list of the
stories in the first edition of The Parent's Assistant,
an edition which is no longer to be found in the British Museum, see Austin Dobson, "The Parent's Assistant," De Libris: Prose and Verse (New York:
Macmillan, 1908), p. 73. Dobson, p. 74, also lists
the stories in the third edition.

12. Dobson, p. 74.

13. M. Edgeworth, XI, 21-25. All future references to
this work and to others in the thirteen-volume series
will be indicated by the volume numbers and page
numbers in parentheses in the body of the text.

14. Darton, p. 143, recognizes Frank's "less human" characteristics, as do other critics.

15. Percy H. Newby, Maria Edgeworth (Denver: Alan Swallow, 1950), p. 39.

16. This dramatic quality is, in this author's opinion, one
of the reasons why Maria's stories are an advance
over the stories written by others prior to these.

17. Florence Valentine Barry, A Century of Children's
Books (New York: George H. Doran Co. , 1923),
p. 181.

18. Annie E. Moore, Literature Old and New for Children
(Boston: Houghton Mifflin Co. , 1934), p. 200. For
more comments on Maria's characters, see Darton,
p. 143-44; and Barry, p. 179, and p. 182.

19. Ibid. , p. 199.

20. Moore, p. 201, points out that Mr. Edgeworth authored

a study of proverbs and maxims; and, consequently, they are often found in the titles and in the stories written by Maria. This observation is quite accurate.

21. Lucas, p. xi-xii.

22. Barry, p. 177.

23. It is interesting, however, that in spite of the highly moralistic nature of The Parent's Assistant, it was reprinted as late as 1948 in the Watergate Classics Series, according to Mary F. Thwaite, From Primer to Pleasure: An Introduction to the History of Children's Books in England, from the Invention of Printing to 1900, with a Chapter on Some Developments Abroad (London: Library Association, 1963), p. 73.

24. Alice Mertz Stevens, "Rousseau's Influence on the Educational Novel" (unpublished Master's thesis, University of Chicago, 1912), p. 39, of Chapter III.

25. Gillian Elise Avery, Nineteenth Century Children: Heroes and Heroines in English Children's Stories, 1780-1900 (London: Hodder and Stoughton, 1965), p. 27.

26. Newby, p. 35.

27. Ibid., p. 35-36.

28. Ibid., p. 36.

29. See footnote 25 above.

30. The lesson the little girl is to learn from this beating is not stated.

31. These points are summarized from Rousseau's letter, cited by R.L. Archer (ed.), Jean-Jacques Rousseau: His Educational Theories Selected from Emile, Julie and Other Writings (Woodbury, N.Y.: Barron's Educational Series, Inc., 1964), p. 239-47.

32. See footnote 24 above.

33. No answer given; sixteen days is this author's answer.

34.   Percival Horace Muir, English Children's Books, 1600-
      1900 (New York: Praeger, 1954), p. 88.

35.   Cornelia Lynde Meigs, "Roots in the Past up to 1840,"
      A Critical History of Children's Literature: A Sur-
      vey of Children's Books in English from Earliest
      Times to the Present, Prepared in 4 pts., ed. Cor-
      nelia L. Meigs (New York: Macmillan, 1953), p.
      105.

Chapter V

Mary Wollstonecraft

Rousseau influenced Mary Wollstonecraft almost as
much as he did Maria Edgeworth; but Maria Edgeworth had
a natural talent for telling stories, whereas Mary Wollstonecraft allowed her desire to teach to overpower her desire to
entertain. The result was that her characters are less human and her stories more didactic.

It is not surprising that the early works of Mary Wollstonecraft were didactic--at that time all children's books
were. She wrote her Thoughts on the Education of Daughters
(1787) after her experience as a teacher in her own school,
which soon closed, and after she tutored the daughters of
Lady Kingsborough. Ralph Wardle, Mary Wollstonecraft's
biographer, points out that this book was written hurriedly
and in a haphazard manner to enable her to get some money
which she needed desperately,[1] and Wardle calls the book "a
collection of innocuous platitudes which any maiden school-
mistress then might have approved."[2] Rousseau also might
have approved most of it, for it certainly seems to echo
some of his ideas. There is no doubt that Mary Wollstonecraft read Rousseau's works because she refers to him and
to his works often in her Vindication of the Rights of Woman
(1792) and occasionally in her letters to Godwin (1796-1797).
Whether she had read Rousseau's Emile before 1787, or
1788, when her Original Stories from Real Life appeared in
print, is the question and one which only internal evidence
can hope to answer.

Thoughts on the Education of Daughters shows some
similarity to Rousseau's Emile. Basically the two are different, however, in that Rousseau sought to educate a boy,
Emile, and Mary Wollstonecraft concerned herself with the
education of girls only. Of course, Rousseau mentions
Sophie, but he is less specific about her education than he
is about Emile's. His somewhat haphazard treatment of
Sophie's education and his belief in the inferiority of women
come under direct attack in the Vindication of the Rights of

101

Woman (1792), but that work comes later than Mary Wollstonecraft's books for children do. In that work, the author
speaks out for a better education for women, her main argument centering around the fact that women deprived of education are deprived both in this world and in the next; for sal-
vation results from virtue, virtue in turn comes from reason,
and reason is acquired at least in part from education.[3] By
1787, however, Mary Wollstonecraft had not yet determined,
or even thought of deciding, what her answer would be to the
question of women's rights or even of men's rights.

Determined from internal evidence only, the influence
of Rousseau on <u>Thoughts on the Education of Daughters</u> seems
strong. As the work was not written for children, it can be
mentioned only briefly, but to show that Rousseau influenced
it would help to prove the point that the book written for children, <u>Original Stories</u>, in the next year, 1788, also shows
Rousseau's influence.[4]

Mary Wollstonecraft begins her books on education by
advocating breast feeding, thus encouraging mothers to take
over their natural responsibility and not push that responsibility off onto nurses.[5] Rousseau felt the same way. Next
Mary Wollstonecraft emphasizes several points, all in accord
with Rousseau's beliefs: the parents should set a good example (5); and the tutors of the child should be inflexible in
the rules they have laid down (6). This last statement seems
to echo Rousseau's idea of "let your 'No,' once uttered, be
a wall of brass."[6]

In the idea of avoiding needless restraint of children
in their early years (7) and in the idea of keeping them a-
way from bad examples (14), Mary Wollstonecraft seems to
agree with Rousseau. She wants children to have a taste for
the beauties of nature and to learn how to think (22). She
feels, as Rousseau did, that memorization without understanding is pointless (25). She permits girls to learn something
of music, drawing, geography, dancing, and elegance of manners, but they should not put too much stress upon these accomplishments (25-27). She differs from Rousseau, however, in that she evidently would not isolate the child since
she says the child should learn "a strict adherence to truth,
a proper submission to superiors; and condescension to inferiors" (21). The last two are in opposition to Rousseau's
views. Rousseau's pupil, because of his isolation, would
not have to deal with either his superiors or his inferiors.
His tutor falls into neither category.

This comparison between Mary Wollstonecraft's
Thoughts on the Education of Daughters and Rousseau's Emile
could be carried further. Only the first three of some
twenty-one chapters have been treated, but this brief comparison should be enough to show that Mary Wollstonecraft
had a great many beliefs in common with Rousseau. She
cites Locke on one occasion (11), but she does not mention
Rousseau directly. It seems more probable that she had
read Emile, however, than that all the above points should
be called coincidence.

The next work that Mary Wollstonecraft wrote for her
publisher, Joseph Johnson,[8] was Original Stories from Real
Life (1788), her first book written for children. Published
again in 1791, it had illustrations by William Blake included.
Rousseau's influence on it will be described in some detail a
little later in this chapter. Following Original Stories, she
translated the Rev. C. G. Salzmann's Elements of Morality
for the Use of Children (1790).[9]

The critic Moses says of Salzmann: "[He] won no
small renown for the excellence of his schools, founded upon
the principles set down by Rousseau."[10] If Mary Wollstonecraft did not know Rousseau's ideas before this time, she
now learned of them. This author believes that she knew of
Rousseau's ideas several years prior to this translation. In
her translation, she has changed all German customs or
opinions to English ones and inserted a tale about Indians.
She calls the translation "a liberal one,"[11] but as she did not
write it originally, it will not be discussed at any length
here.[12] Her "Introductory Address to Parents," included a-
long with her translation reveals one of her fundamental beliefs, one which not only coincides with Rousseau's belief,
but also appears to be the principle in illustration of which
most children's stories were written:

> If, for example, to make a child have an aversion
> for idleness, I say to him, idleness, my dear child
> is a vice: it makes a man discontented, injures
> his health, and ruins his circumstances, this dis-
> course, I believe, would not have much effect; for
> the child cannot form a right idea of discontent,
> health, or circumstances: but if I say to him,
> there was once a farmer, named Brown, who was
> a very idle man, and describe him; as he is drawn
> in chap. 16, Vol. I. I shall certainly give birth
> to a wish, at least, not to be idle; for his imagina-

tion representing idleness in so lively a manner,
in the picture of Brown, he will feel uneasiness inseparable from it; but, should I go still further,
and shew him Brown in the print, saying now view
yourself this poor wretch, see how he sits there,
half asleep, as if he were sick--how miserable is
his whole appearance! what a shabby coat he has
on, and what an object of compassion is the horse!
Seeing thus the wretchedness which springs from
idleness with his own eyes, his whole heart must
rise against it. (xiv-xv)

Original Stories from Real Life

This principle for writing children's stories appears
again and again in Mary Wollstonecraft's Original Stories
from Real Life, the purpose of which is seen in its subtitle,
With Conversations, Calculated to Regulate the Affections,
and Form the Mind to Truth and Goodness. Mary Wollstonecraft set a task for herself that differs from Rousseau's in
that Rousseau takes the newborn child and educates him;
whereas she attempts to correct the errors in an older child's
education. Harvey Darton says that in this work she gives:

> her own views of regulation, truth and goodness,
> quite as much as following a philosophy of the time
> or of any particular thinker; though her translation
> of Salzmann has caused her to be identified to some
> extent with his general school or doctrine. [13]

Mary Wollstonecraft does give her own views, but I believe
those views show some influence which she felt before she
translated Salzmann's book and became associated with his
school, which was, of course, based on Rousseau's teachings.

Mary Wollstonecraft states in the "Preface" such ideas
as not permitting children to be bound with the fetters of
habit, [14] opposing false politeness, imparting knowledge by
example rather than by teaching (iv), and recognizing that
every child has an individual bent (v). All of these views
are in accord with Rousseau's. She also states in the "Preface" a point which differs somewhat from Rousseau's thinking: the child should learn about God (vi). Rousseau did
not oppose girls having some knowledge of God, but he does
not put the emphasis on God that Mary Wollstonecraft does.

Rousseau's influence on the characters of <u>Original Sto-
ries from Real Life</u> appears to be stronger in the character
of Mrs. Mason than in any other character. Virtually every
critic of this period in children's literature has mentioned
Mrs. Mason. One critic calls her "a female super-Barlow,"[15]
another calls her "the female counterpart of the perfect tutor,"[16] and still another says she is "Mr. Barlow in petti-
coats."[17] These critics obviously see the similarity between
Day's Barlow and Mrs. Mason, whom Mary Wollstonecraft
obviously modeled after Rousseau's tutor. No one to my
knowledge, however, has made a direct connection between
Mrs. Mason and Emile's tutor. There is a connection.

Mrs. Mason is like Emile's tutor in that she is always with her pupils and she always knows everything. Also
like Emile's tutor, she uses deceit and even lies to get her
point across. For example, she allows Caroline, one of the
two children under her care, to spend all her money foolishly
on toys. Then Mary Wollstonecraft says: "When Mrs. Mason found [Caroline's money] was all expended, she looked
round for an object in distress; a poor woman soon presented
herself" (161). Caroline, of course, cannot help the woman
since she has spent her money foolishly.[18] Mrs. Mason
says after this incident: "I am glad that this accident has
occurred, to prove to you, that prodigality and generosity
are incompatible" (164). It was obviously no accident; it was
an episode contrived to teach Caroline, although the part a-
bout the woman's needing help was not contrived.

Mrs. Mason uses the techniques of giving examples
and stating morals, as well as having children actually experience what she wishes them to learn. Rousseau, of
course, favored the last method and had Emile learn everything the hard way, by experience. Mrs. Mason believes in
learning by experience also, but she cannot resist stating
morals to emphasize the lesson just experienced. She goes
a step further than the tutor who allowed Emile to catch a
cold because he was in a draft caused by the wind coming
through a window he broke. Mrs. Mason does not allow physical discomfort or illness to result from her pupils' ignor-
ance, but she is merciless when it comes to causing mental
anguish. On one occasion when the children misbehave, she
says: "I give you to-night a kiss of peace, an affectionate
one you have not deserved" (48). Mary, Mrs. Mason's other
pupil, tells Caroline after Mrs. Mason leaves the room that
she cannot sleep because "I am afraid of Mrs. Mason's eyes"
(50).

Unlike Emilie's tutor, Mrs. Mason teaches morals
with a vengeance. In trying to teach the children not to harm
insects even if they are sometimes troublesome, she says to
Mary and Caroline: "You are often troublesome--I am
stronger than you--yet I do not kill you" (4). About the highest compliment Mrs. Mason pays the girls is telling them
they "have acted like rational creatures" (10).[19] To teach
the lesson on tenderheartedness, Mrs. Mason tells of a man
who was not tenderhearted; she says:

> When he became a father, he not only neglected to
> educate his children, and set them a good example,
> but he taught them to be cruel while he tormented
> them: the consequence was, that they neglected
> him when he was old and feeble; and he died in a
> ditch. (17)

Even though she gives negative examples, Mrs. Mason
has the same criticism of the man in the story cited above
as Rousseau would have of him: he did not educate his children; and he did not set a good example.

Mary Wollstonecraft's governess cannot resist the
kind of story stated above, and she has several for almost
every occasion. She cites an example of a pig when Caroline is guilty of overeating (71). In teaching Mary about procrastination, she cites the example of Mrs. Dowdy, who is
always keeping others waiting for her (90), but this example
is mild compared to an earlier one on procrastination. This
example will be drawn in more detail because it shows Mrs.
Mason at her best, and her best, in this case, contrasts
with Rousseau's tutor; for there is nothing she will not try
in order to prove her point. Rousseau's tutor uses deceit,
but he is not the extremist that Mrs. Mason is. She is a
"gorgon" to use E. V. Lucas's epithet,[20] or a "heartless vi-
rago" to use another critic's term,[21] or in the words of
Florence Barry: "Nothing softer than granite could suggest
her outline."[22]

Mrs. Mason's story concerns Charles Townley, a man
given to procrastination. He has no profession, and he whiles
away his wealth until he finally lands in jail. A friend offers
to help him; the friend pays Charles' debts, and Charles
sets sail for the East Indies. After fifteen years, Charles
amasses enough wealth to return to England and repay his
friend. The friend has by this time, through no fault of his
own, fallen into debt and is in prison. Charles delays going

to aid his friend; when he finally goes, he learns the friend
has died the day before.

Since the death may not be enough to teach Charles a
lesson, Mrs. Mason quotes the following letter, written to
Charles by the dying man:

> I have been reduced by unforeseen misfortunes; yet
> when I heard of your arrival, a gleam of joy
> cheered by heart--I thought I knew your's, and that
> my latter days might still have been made comfort-
> able in your society, for I loved you; I even ex-
> pected pleasure; but I was mistaken; death is my
> only friend. (84)

Rousseau would have been touched by this letter as he was
an extremely sentimental, emotional man; but it is unlikely
that he would have approved of this tear-jerking technique
for teaching children.

Mrs. Mason, however, is not through yet. After
reading the letter, Charles resolves to do something for his
friend's daughter. Procrastination is difficult to cure, however, and Charles does nothing for awhile. When he finally
does see the daughter, he learns that her lover was sent to
sea by his family. His family did not want him to marry a
girl with no money. The poor girl is left destitute; she
marries an old rake who makes her life so miserable that
because of him and her other misfortunes, she loses her
mind. Her husband commits her. Charles takes her from
the madhouse and provides for her. She is a constant re-
minder to him until he dies. Being responsible for the death
of a friend and the insanity of the friend's daughter are very
heavy burdens to bear, and Charles seems much more guilty
than young Mary is of procrastination. Mrs. Mason is re-
lentless, however, much more so than Rousseau's tutor.

The other characters, Mary and Caroline, are as
Florence Barry describes them: "mere wax tablets whereon
[Mrs. Mason] records her impressions of virtue. Their very
faults are placed upon them like labels, for Mrs. Mason to
remove."[23] They are merely little girls whose education has
been neglected prior to Mrs. Mason's arrival. There is little evidence to show that they are following in the tradition
of Rousseau's Sophie. Ralph Wardle points out that the two
writers did not agree on the development of certain attributes
of Sophie's character; he says:

Mary [Wollstonecraft] resented [Rousseau's] picture of
Sophie as one whose mind is 'pleasing but not brilliant,
and thorough but not deep,' who finds needlework to be
the occupation best suited to her talents, and who
passively accepts the religion chosen for her by
those wiser than herself.[24]

In keeping with this disagreement, Mary and Caroline
sew some clothes for poor people (101), but do not do needlework often; they are actively taught religion, although they
are seldom permitted to read the Bible because they are too
young to understand it (12). It was for a similar reason that
Rousseau wished Emile to have no exposure to religion at an
early age.

Some characters are merely personfications of their
main characteristic. Generally, these characters are distin-
guishable by their names which are in the humours tradition:
Jane Fretful, Lady Sly, Mrs. Trueman, Mrs. Dowdy, and
Mr. Lofty.[25] All of these characters have small roles in
the book; none show to any extent the effect of Rousseau's
doctrine, except perhaps Mrs. Trueman. Mary Wollstonecraft, however, appears to have used Rousseau's ideas more
in her concept of a governess than anywhere else.

Rousseau's influence on plot is practically negligible
except for the episodes which demonstrate a punishment suited to the crime. One example occurs when Caroline eats
too much and gets sick, a fitting punishment but not one pre-
scribed by Mrs. Mason. One that she does dole out occurs
on this same occasion while Caroline is sick. Mary and
Mrs. Mason leave Caroline at home and go to Mrs. Good-
win's garden where they pick and eat fruit. Caroline misses
both the visit and the fruit.

The plot follows Rousseau's teachings in one other
way. It is a series of episodes, constructed to give the children the lessons they need at a particular time. Rousseau
had said that if the tutor uses a book of fables, he should
never read it in the order written; rather, the tutor should
select a fable for his pupil which is directly applicable to
the situation the child is in at the time.

The subjects treated by Mary Wollstonecraft also fit
the situations the children find themselves in, and the subjects show the effects of Rousseau's ideas more than the plot
or even the characters do. For example, the subject of

fashion comes up in the education of girls. Mary Wollstonecraft's views here are quite similar to Rousseau's. Mrs.
Mason says of Mrs. Trueman, who is a model of goodness
in the book: "She did not implicitly follow the reigning fashion, for she had learned to distinguish, and in the most trivial matters acted according to the dictates of good taste"
(58). Mrs. Mason tells Caroline: "immoderate fondness for
dress, I term vanity" (91) and warns her not to be "too solic-
itous to conform to the changing fashions" (92). Like Rousseau, Mrs. Mason feels neatness is most important; and also like Rousseau, she has no objection to the girls dressing
in gay colors (94).

      Mary Wollstonecraft follows Rousseau in the ideas of
the mother nursing her own child (108), of being kind to animals (6-7), of treating servants kindly, and that the more
one depends upon servants, the less admirable he is (97).
This last point is seen when young Mary gets angry at her
maid and asks the maid if she knows whom she is speaking
to. Mrs. Mason answers: "to a little girl, who is only as-
sisted because she is weak" (90). Rousseau might have made
exactly the same answer in the same situation. This attitude
toward servants cannot be attributed solely to Rousseau's influence, but it is another attitude the two writers have in
common.

      These two authors also have similar beliefs about the
importance of the so-called accomplishments of young ladies.
They are in Mrs. Mason's words : "cultivated to render us
pleasing to our domestic friends," but she continues: "virtue
is necessary; it must ever be the foundation of our peace
and usefulness" (144). And girls should be useful, Mrs. Mason stresses, not only to help others, but also to please
themselves (102). Gossiping is not only useless, but it is in
poor taste, so Mrs. Mason cautions her pupils. Rousseau
would agree.

      Mary Wollstonecraft does not agree with Rousseau on
everything, however, for she has the girls read at a much
younger age than Emile (101). It is interesting that one of
the books they read is Mrs. Trimmer's Fabulous Histories,
a book which will be discussed in Chapter VII. In regard to
that book, Mrs. Mason, true to Rousseau's anti-fable or
anti-fairy doctrine, stresses to the girls that they must understand that the birds, who are the main characters of the
book, cannot really talk (46-47). [26]

Mrs. Mason wishes the girls to learn good habits in regard to their Heavenly Father (137), and she emphasizes the dependence of the girls on other people and on God (136-37). In both of these ideas she is stating a view different from that of Rousseau. Rousseau, however, did not oppose Sophie's learning religion or her being dependent upon her husband; it was only in regard to Emile's education that he emphasized complete independence.

Rousseau and Mary Wollstonecraft would agree basically on the parting advice that Mrs. Mason gives to her pupils. Rousseau would probably not, however, emphasize religion to Sophie as much as the following speech does:

> Avoid anger; exercise compassion; and love truth. Recollect, that from religion your chief comfort must spring, and never neglect the duty of prayer. Learn from experience the comfort that arises from making known your wants and sorrows to the wisest and best of Beings, in whose hands are the issues, not only of this life, but of that which is to come. (167)

Mary Wollstonecraft appears to have had many views compatible with Rousseau's. In most cases, they are views to which any educator might subscribe, such as vanity and gossip are undesirable; truth, generosity and charity are desirable. Yet there are so many points of similarity in the concept of the tutor, or governess, and in the educational ideas stated in <u>Thoughts on the Education of Daughters</u> that it seems too much of a coincidence to say Mary Wollstonecraft did not feel Rousseau's influence. I believe she did. She was obviously aware of the other writers of children's books of the period--Mrs. Barbauld and Sarah Trimmer are mentioned specifically--and there were probably others whom she had read. It is, therefore, quite likely that she had read the educational philosophers also. It is less likely, however, that Dorothy Kilner, or her sister Mary Jane Kilner, had read Rousseau; but they, along with Lady Eleanor Fenn, are the subjects of the next chapter.

Notes

1. Ralph M. Wardle, <u>Mary Wollstonecraft: A Critical Biography</u> (Lawrence, Kansas: University of Kansas Press, 1951), p. 48.

2. Ralph M. Wardle, "Mary Wollstonecraft, Analytical Reviewer," PMLA, LXII (1947), 1000.

3. George E. G. Catlin in his "Introduction" to Mary Wollstonecraft, The Rights of Woman, in The Rights of Woman by Mary Wollstonecraft and the Subjection of Women by John Stuart Mill (London: J. M. Dent, 1929), p. 15, summarizes the main argument of this book as does Wardle, Biography, p. 153.

4. By 1793, the year after the Vindication, Mary Wollstonecraft met Gilbert Imlay, who was to become her lover and the father of her first child, Fanny. It is interesting that this man who so captured Mary Wollstonecraft's affections is described by Wardle, Biography, p. 184, as "an unspoiled child of nature, an incarnation of Rousseau's Emile."

5. Mary Wollstonecraft, Thoughts on the Education of Daughters: With Reflections on Female Conduct, in the More Important Duties of Life (London: Printed for J. Johnson, 1787), p. 3. All future references to this work will be indicated by the page numbers in parentheses in the body of the text.

6. See, p. 18, for the complete quotation.

7. Because this book is rare, a listing will be made of the other eighteen chapter headings in addition to The Nursery, Moral Discipline, and Exterior Accomplishments so that the reader will have a better idea of the nature of this book: Artifical Manners; Dress; The Fine Arts; Reading; Boarding-Schools; The Temper; Unfortunate Situation of Females, fashionably educated, and left without a fortune; Love; Matrimony; Desultory Thoughts; The Benefits Which Arise from Disappointments; On the Treatment of Servants; Observance of Sunday; On the Misfortune of Flucuating Principles; Benevolence; Card-Playing; The Theatre; and Public Places.

8. Johnson appears to have entertained at some time many of the well-known writers of his time; Wardle, Biography, p. 126, cites Priestly, Price, Mrs. Barbauld, Paine, Godwin, Blake, and Mary Wollstonecraft.

9. Wardle, Biography, p. 316, points out the interesting
    fact the Rev. Salzmann translated William Godwin's
    Memoirs of Mary Wollstonecraft Godwin into German
    in 1799.

10. Montrose J. Moses, Children's Books and Reading (New
    York: Mitchell Kennerley, 1907), p. 97n.

11. Christian Gotthilf Salzmann, Elements of Morality for
    the Use of Children: With an Introductory Address
    to Parents, trans. Mary Wollstonecraft (2 vols.;
    Philadelphia: Hoff and Kammerar, 1796), I, vi.
    All future references will be to Volume I, thus only
    the page numbers will be given in parentheses in the
    body of the text.

12. It would, however, be interesting to trace Rousseau's
    influence on German stories for children.

13. F. J. Harvey Darton, Children's Books in England:
    Five Centuries of Social Life (Cambridge at the Uni-
    versity Press, 1932), p. 203.

14. Mary Wollstonecraft, Original Stories from Real Life:
    With Conversations, Calculated to Regulate the Affec-
    tions, and Form the Mind to Truth and Goodness
    (London: Printed by J. Crowder for J. Johnson,
    1800), p. iii. All future references to this work will
    be indicated by the page numbers in parentheses in
    the body of the text.

15. Darton, p. 203.

16. Mary F. Thwaite, From Primer to Pleasure: An In-
    troduction to the History of Children's Books in Eng-
    land, from the Invention of Printing to 1900, with a
    Chapter on Some Developments Abroad (London: Li-
    brary Association, 1963), p. 71.

17. Agnes Repplier, A Happy Half-Century and Other Es-
    says (Boston: Houghton Mifflin, 1908), p. 159.

18. In this action, she certainly is similar to Maria Edge-
    worth's Rosamond.

19. Thwaite, p. 71, points out the governess is merely ex-
    pressing "the commonly held belief that children were

a lower form of human life.

20. E. V. Lucas, "Preface," to reproduction of Mary Woll-
     stonecraft, Original Stories from Real Life (London:
     Henry Froude, 1906), cited by Thwaite, p. 71.

21. Wardle, Biography, p. 88.

22. Florence Valentine Barry, A Century of Children's
     Books (New York: George H. Doran Co., 1923),
     p. 116.

23. Ibid.

24. Wardle, Biography, p. 148.

25. The humours tradition of naming characters, used by
     Bunyan and others, was also used by Sarah Fielding
     in The Governess (1749); and it is because of her,
     in part, that the tradition continued in children's lit-
     erature.

26. Mary Wollstonecraft had also read Mrs. Barbauld's
     works for children, for she mentions them in
     Thoughts on the Education of Daughters, (17). It is
     interesting that one episode of Original Stories, that
     of Jane Fretful's kicking a chair or a table when she
     is angry (29), appears very similar to an episode in
     Lessons for Children from Two to Four Years Old,
     p. 85-89. One idea in Original Stories also shows
     a striking similarity to Lady Fenn's The Fair Spec-
     tator; or The Invisible Monitor; that is, Mrs. Mason
     tells her pupils not to conceal any falsehood because
     the Searcher of hearts sees everything (35). Lady
     Fenn's book is based upon the idea of an invisible
     spectator monitoring everything.

Chapter VI

Lady Eleanor Fenn, the Kilner Sisters

Lady Eleanor Fenn and the Kilner sisters had at least two things in common: their publisher was John Marshall, and they wrote during the 1780's. Although Rousseau's ideas were popular then, all three writers seem to have taken little note of him. Lady Fenn introduced her Fables with a quote from him which says that in effect the impressions made on a child's mind are there for life.[1] At least one critic dates the Fables 1783; and if she is correct, the Fables preceded Lady Fenn's other books for children: Cobwebs to Catch Flies (1783?), The Fairy Spectator (1788?), The Juvenile Tatler (1789).[2] Thus Lady Fenn would at least have been aware of Rousseau before she wrote her children's books.

There is less evidence to show that the Kilner sisters were aware of Rousseau. They wrote a number of children's books, usually under the initials "M.P." and "S.S." "M.P." was Dorothy Kilner, and "S.S." was Mary Jane Kilner. Some critics have said that "M.P." stood for Maryland Point, the hometown of the sisters.[3] Others have said the initials stood for the pseudonym Mary Pelham.[4] No critic comments on the "S.S." of Mary Jane Kilner. Virtually nothing is known about the two sisters' lives, but their writings are important enough to deserve mention by all serious students of the history of children's literature. Other authors of children's books of the time cited their works also.[5] The works which have been selected as typical are The Life and Perambulation of a Mouse, Anecdotes of a Boarding-School, and The Village School by Dorothy Kilner and The Adventures of a Pincusion, Memoirs of a Peg-Top, and Jemima Placid by Mary Jane Kilner.[6] There is no way of knowing whether the Kilners read Rousseau except by internal evidence from their stories. A discussion of what internal evidence there is will be found at the conclusion of the comments on Lady Fenn's books.

A little more is known about Lady Fenn than is known

114

about the Kilners. She, like the Kilners, often used a pseudonym; the most common ones she used were Mrs. Teachwell
and Mrs. Lovechild.[7] Darton points out that she and her
husband, John Fenn, were childless; she thus wrote for her
nieces and nephews, and she actually made her books, bind-
ing, and all.[8] Her interest in, and love of, children is evident in her works, but at the same time the didactic element is also ever-present.

Cobwebs to Catch Flies

One critic has described Lady Fenn's purpose in writing Cobwebs to Catch Flies as: "Tempt your child into the
web first, she felt, and a year or two later you will be able
to start gorging him with information and reforming his character."[9] This criticism seems harsh; yet it is close to the
truth. The subtitle gives an idea of what Lady Fenn had in
mind: Dialogues in Short Sentences, Adapted for Children
from the Age of Three to Eight Years. She states in the
"Advertisement" that the mothers who read her book will ex-
cuse any faults which arise from confining the language to
short words. The first volume of Cobwebs to Catch Flies
consists of words three to six letters long for children between three and five years old. The second volume has no
such restriction; yet the words are still quite simple and
short.

Lady Fenn further claims that she has mentioned nothing but objects with which the child is absolutely familiar.
In this idea she follows Mrs. Barbauld's Lessons for Children. Lady Fenn also says she has included no thoughts or
words beyond the comprehension of the child. In this she
agrees with Rousseau who opposed the child's being exposed
to thoughts or words beyond his grasp.

There is some similarity between Rousseau's characters and those in Cobwebs to Catch Flies. The pupil in the
latter work is not a single character, but a number of boys
and girls who learn about many things. The role of the tutor
is also played by many people--Mamma, Papa, Grandpapa,
Mr. and Mrs. Freelove, Mr. Steady, Mrs. Lovechild, and
even some of the boys and girls themselves. There are a
total of twenty-five stories in both volumes; a few are continued ones. In this way, Lady Fenn presents lessons which
are pertinent to a wide range of children; Rousseau chose to
take one child and show his development and lessons in a

chronological order. In this book, as in The Fairy Spectator and The Juvenile Tatler, Lady Fenn uses the humours tradition for naming many of her characters.

In general, the stories are dialogues; the children usually bombard their tutor with questions. Rousseau wished Emile to be inquisitive, for his own curiosity would give him the desire to learn, a desire Rousseau felt was important. Though the children are similar, there are two characters in the first volume who are in opposition to Rousseau's tutor. Those two are Mamma in "The Dog" and Maid in "The Farm-Yard." In the former, Mamma explains to Boy what the dog says when he wags his tail. On one occasion he says, according to Mamma: "Pray let me go; I wish to go with you."[10] On another occasion, Mamma claims he says: "I love you; you have a cake, and I have none: will you not be good to me? Will you not give some of your cake to your poor dog?" (I, 23) The concept of attributing words to a dog's tail was quite unusual in this period of realism in children's stories. In the story of "The Farm-Yard," Maid tells Boy that the pigs cry to her for food. "They say, as well as they can, 'Pray feed me, pray feed me; do pray feed me!'" (I, 29)

Thus, Lady Fenn was one of the first in this period to attribute words to animals; the Kilner sisters do also, even giving the power of speech to inanimate objects, but they are careful to apologize for such action and to make sure the children realize that animals and objects cannot really talk. Sarah Trimmer also uses the device of having birds talk, and Mary Wollstonecraft is careful to have Mrs. Mason point out to her pupils that birds cannot really talk.[11] Lady Fenn, then, opposes Rousseau directly, for she does not apologize; yet she never has the dog or the pig speak himself. Instead the tutor-figure explains the desires of the animals.

The characters in the second volume show more development. In the opening story a gentleman's son learns from a farmer's son in a manner reminiscent of the main characters in Sandford and Merton, the first volume of that book appearing at approximately the same time as this one. Also the character of Mrs. Lovechild appears in Volume II. She is much like Mrs. Teachwell, who appears in the discussion of Lady Fenn's other works. Both believe in books for children suited to their ages; Mrs. Lovechild also believes in toys which can both improve and amuse children (I, 47). In

this regard she appears to be a precursor of Maria Edgeworth's Madame de Rosier in "The Good French Governess."
Rousseau believed toys should improve; although he never mentioned toys outright, he did think the magnetic duck Emile
saw was good for teaching him about magnets. In addition
to playing with toys, he felt that the playing of musical instruments and various sports were good for the physical development of the child.

Lady Fenn is not consistent in her techniques. Sometimes she follows Rousseau, as when she uses specific examples. Other times she states morals as when a little boy
cannot make up his mind and his mother says: "If you get
the trick to like now this, now that, and now you know not
what, it will do you harm all your life. So it is, that boys
and men spend too much; so it is, that they act like fools"
(I, 52). Also unlike Rousseau, Lady Fenn uses reason on
the child. Mama answers Boy's question in "The Morning" a-
bout time to get up by telling him six is the time to get up
and go out, for by ten it will be too hot (I, 13).

In regard to the plot, Volume I has no real development of story line; Volume II has more continuity and also
shows some evidence of Rousseau's teaching devices when a
young child chances upon an object, giving his parent an opportunity to teach the child. For example, the little boy in
"The Spider" finds a spider; his mother teaches him about
spiders and about other insects as a result (II, 22-23).

In the second volume there are two examples of Rousseau's idea about punishment. One occurs when a boy goes
on a ride at the fair after being told not to; the coach in
which he rides breaks and he hurts his leg badly (II, 37-38).
The other example happens when Miss Wilful teases a dog
until he bites her. Mr. Steady's lecture to her goes un-
heeded, for she resolves to get a thick glove and then tease
the dog again (II, 45). She is one of the few children in any
of these stories who is permitted to continue her obstinate
behavior. She appears to be that rare child about whom
Rousseau spoke when he said that once a child wills to do
wrong, all hope is lost for him. [12]

Many of the subjects Lady Fenn treats are the same
ones Rousseau taught. There are numerous examples of kindness to animals (I, 11, 44, 48; II, 19, 11, 49-50) and generosity (I, 13, 23; II, 6). Both authors stress internal beauty over external (II, 49). Lady Fenn seems to follow Rous-

seau specifically in the idea that if little girls have dolls,
they will want to make clothes for them and thus can be encouraged to learn to sew (I, 35, 60-61), and in the praise of
a child's learning a little about gardening (II, 6, 31-32) and
about botany (I, 57). Lady Fenn felt understanding of the
written word was important for the child, just as Rousseau
felt it was; yet the children in "The Useful Play" do memorize. They memorize passages in prose, not verse. Lady
Fenn evidently felt as Mrs. Barbauld did that most verse was
beyond the comprehension of children.

Mrs. Barbauld's brother, John Aikin, may in turn
have taken an episode from Lady Fenn. Lady Fenn has an
example of a young girl who has only worn clothes for her
doll because she has spent her crown to help a poor child
who had no clothes (I, 62). Aikin in his story "Half-a-
Crown" has a young boy lectured to about spending his money
wisely. [13] Aikin may have followed Lady Fenn's lead in explaining such things as the making of cloth and describing the
various kinds of leaves from trees (I, 55), for he often explains processes and describes plants. These two authors
seem on such occasions to forget to be didactic. Rousseau
would have approved of this forgetfulness, for his interest
was in the child's acquiring knowledge as well as morality.

Lady Fenn differs from Rousseau in her belief that
young children should have books (II, 3), and that fables are
good for teaching children; Rousseau, of course, did not entirely oppose fables for teaching. Lady Fenn has the two little girls in "The Useful Play" learn about teaching words to
others through various word games (II, 58-63). Although
Rousseau does not suggest games, he probably would not have
opposed them for Emile; he felt, however, that girls seldom
had a desire to learn to read or write.

Thus, in a number of ways Lady Fenn agrees with
Rousseau, but as the discussion of her other books shows,
she disagrees about fairies and is by no means a devoted fol-
lower of Rousseau. Both The Fairy Spectator and The Juvenile Tatler repeat some of the same ideas as Cobwebs to
Catch Flies, but they appear to have been written for a little
older child.

The Fairy Spectator

Many people besides Rousseau opposed tales about

fairies. Lady Fenn was no doubt aware of this opposition;
and, as a consequence, she, as Mrs. Teachwell, says to
Miss Sprightly: "I will write you a dialogue, in which the
Fairy shall converse; and I will give you a moral for your
dream.--You know that stories of Fairies are all fabulous?"[14]
Once her readers are sufficiently cautioned that the story
that follows is fictitious, Lady Fenn feels free to write the
story of her invisible monitor.[15] In her dedication she prepared the way for the fairy by appealing to the child's belief
about God. She says: "There is an Eye which sees us
wherever we are" (iv). It would appear that she has taken
the concept of an awe-inspiring God who sees and knows all
and reduced that vision to that of a delightful fairy who would
have more appeal for young children. Rousseau claimed
young children could not understand the concept of God, thus
boys should not learn about God until they could understand,
and girls may learn very young since they will never truly
understand. In either case, both boys and girls could understand the fairy, although the story is obviously written for
girls. The concept of a fairy's guiding them is more in
keeping with the child's understanding; and since the fairy
stands for all that is good, Lady Fenn no doubt hoped there
would be no objection to her character.

The fairy's story is the creation of the imagination of
Mrs. Teachwell, who is the governess to the girls and the
narrator of much of The Fairy Spectator, although she lets
the fairy speak for her. The fairy is virtually unaffected by
Rousseau's tutor; about the only similarity is that the two
contrive vivid ways by which to teach their pupils--Emile's
tutor uses deceit; the fairy uses magic.

The Fairy Spectator: or, The Invisible Monitor is
unlike any other book of its time that this author has seen in
its use of magic. There is a magic mirror in which the
owner may see on one side what she is and on the other side
what she ought to be. There is a magic locket set with rubies. The rubies change color as the wearer feels any of
the following undesirable feelings: envy, anger, timidity,
niggardliness, or jealousy. The third of the magical objects
is a rose which has a thorn which pricks its owner whenever
she does something wrong. It is difficult to say what Rousseau's reaction would have been to the use of magic, even
for a didactic purpose. He certainly has his tutor use tricks
and deceits, but none of them fall under the category of the
unreal or imaginative. It is more likely that he would have
approved of the lessons taught but not of the techniques used.

Lady Fenn uses some of Rousseau's techniques, however, for she uses comparison and example (with the mirror
which shows both good and bad) and experience (with the
locket and thorn). For example, when Miss Child, the re-
cipient of the locket and the rose, behaves properly, she
feels "unspeakable satisfaction" (57), which the fairy explains
by saying that Miss Child could not "have conceived an idea
of the complacency attending a consciousness of doing well--
of obliging and pleasing by acts of beneficience, till [she]
had experienced it" (58).

Rousseau had no obvious effect on plot; there are a
few episodes of virtue rewarded that are in direct opposition
to Rousseau's teaching. Miss Child, the main subject of one
of the interpolated stories, undergoes three tests. The fairy,
who has watched over her and given her the mirror and the
locket, offers her a choice of a purse which would always be
full of money, a bonnet which could convey her anywhere she
desires, or a ring which would make her invisible (59).
Miss Child gives such admirable answers in refusing all
three gifts that the fairy rewards her by appointing Miss
Child her companion and changing Miss Child's name to Amiable. She gives Amiable the job of guardian to Mrs. Teachwell's children with the power of assuming whatever shape
she desires (62-63).

Miss Child had no way of knowing she was to receive
such a reward. Thus Lady Fenn stresses the admirable answer of Miss Child and the true goodness of her character.
Rousseau was never quick to reward; nor does he ever emphasize external beauty which I believe Lady Fenn does un-
consciously. She stresses the fact that external advantages
are often misleading (22); yet when Amiable assumes the
shape of a fairy, Lady Fenn describes her as:

> stately like the queen of Fairies on a court day:
> yet her garment, though it seemed so full, did not
> conceal the beauty of her figure, which was so del-
> icately formed, that description can give little idea
> of it. Upon her head she wore a coronet of dia-
> monds, emeralds, and rubies. (74)

Later she assumes an even more beautiful appearance. This
time the coronet of jewels has given way to "the most delicate flowers" (75). The flowers, articles of nature, are
more in accord with Rousseau, but still the emphasis is on
external beauty, which Lady Fenn earlier cautioned her readers about.

The subjects the fairy teaches Miss Child are to moderate her temper, to be generous, and to be charitable (37). Miss Child, as Amiable, later teaches Miss Playful to avoid pride, envy, and vanity (81). All these subjects are in keeping with those Sophie learned, but they are those which any well-educated young lady of the time would learn. Such ideas as an emphasis on neatness and on a plain and modest manner (45), a praise of needlework (47), and an aversion to ornaments, such as jewelry (51) sound more specifically like Rousseau's ideas.

There are a few more subjects which both Rousseau and Lady Fenn treated, but not in the same manner. Rousseau stressed the desire to learn on the child's part; Lady Fenn urges a desire to improve on the child's part. Both Sophie and Lady Fenn's character, Miss Sprightly, learn about God; Miss Sprightly, however, seems to pray more. Rousseau opposed books for young boys and felt young girls were not interested in reading; Lady Fenn gives her girls books to read. Thus the two authors differ; yet both stress material suited to the age of the child, Lady Fenn in speaking of books (25-54) and Rousseau in speaking of topics suitable for Emile's tutor to teach his young pupil.

Lady Fenn changes her techniques and subjects somewhat when she writes The Juvenile Tatler. Although Mrs. Teachwell appears again, she is far less active in the role of governess for her girls, for The Juvenile Tatler has a different format.

The Juvenile Tatler

The Juvenile Tatler is a collection of five moral dialogues and dramas: "The Foolish Mother," "The Prudent Daughter," "The Innocent Romp," "The Wife," and "The Wary Mother." They are obviously directed towards educating girls. Lady Fenn under the pseudonym of Mrs. Teachwell uses the device later used by John Aikin in Evenings at Home;[16] that is, the pupils write stories which they put in an urn. The stories are later drawn and discussed. Lady Fenn says, in part:

> It may reasonably be supposed, that the opening of this collection was expected with some impatience; and that few of the family would choose to be absent when notice was given that some of its contents

were to be divulged.[17]

The five dramas listed above are five of those selected by Mrs. Teachwell from the urn. In each case the purpose is improvement of the pupils, which Mrs. Teachwell hopes to accomplish "by strewing the paths of literature with flowers" (v).

The first drama, "The Foolish Mother," is an eleven-page dialogue between Mrs. Giddy and Mrs. Steady. Mrs. Giddy is the foolish mother of two boys who, because she is not firm, cannot govern them as well as Mrs. Steady governs her ten children. Mrs. Steady echoes Rousseau when she says she never changes her no to yes (4).[18] She also speaks of an idea which Rousseau did not believe in. She says to Mrs. Giddy: "Alas, madame! You neglected the dawn of evil passions, and now you see your error" (6). Rousseau, of course, believed the child was free from original sin; at the same time, however, he isolated Èmile from all except his tutor. It seems inevitable that if there are two children, there will be conflict; for neither of the children would have the ability to solve problems in the ways of Emile's tutor.

Mrs. Giddy threatens her boys when they do not mind her. She tells them she will take little Catherine (evidently their baby sister) home from the nurse; she will no longer care for them and even may send them to school to be whipped (9). Rousseau would have opposed the threat technique much as Mrs. Steady does; Mrs. Steady has some ideas in common with Rousseau, but most of them fall in the realm of common sense, such as telling Mrs. Giddy that her threat will plant envy, jealousy, and dislike of school in the boys (10). Mrs. Steady also opposes tyranny, oppression, and cruelty (7-8), again, subjects about which Rousseau felt the same way; but there is nothing in "The Foolish Wife" that is uniquely Rousseau's idea.

The second drama is another short dialogue, again showing ideas which coincide with Rousseau's, but which may or may not have had their origin in Emile. The dialogue is between Miss Sneer and Miss Warner; the latter is the prudent daughter. The action, though slight, centers around Mr. Fop's ball. Miss Warner's mother was not invited; and since she did not go, she did not want her daughter to go unescorted (15-16). Miss Sneer says the real reason is Mrs. Warner's mortification at not being invited (16); she also

claims that Miss Warner must have had an unpleasant evening at home (18); her last sneering remark to Miss Warner
is, in part: "there were no attempts to carry us off by
force to Scotland" (19).

Miss Warner then states a maxim, one which Rousseau would advocate for Sophie, but one which he would not
merely state. He would have Miss Sneer get carried off to
Scotland to learn by experience, not by maxim. Miss Warner says: "A prudent girl will never venture into mixed com-
panies of young people, but under the protection of some
woman of fashion and character" (20). The dialogue ends
with the two girls parting company, Miss Warner having re-
fused Miss Sneer's invitation to go outside to see Mr. Fop
and Mr. Strut. Obviously, Miss Sneer has learned nothing
from mere stated moral.

The "Innocent Romp," a drama with the lead taken by
a Miss Briskly, shows no evidence of Rousseau's influence,
but it is significant because it contains the first truly mis-
chievous girl character. Florence Barry gives Lady Fenn
credit for realistic characters in this drama, and praises
Lady Fenn for Miss Briskly especially: "She invents amusing
pranks for her heroine, and is original in admitting a girl to
the masculine pastime of mischief."[19]

The fourth selection concerns Sir Charles Freeman,
who is looking for a wife. Two flirtatious ladies--Miss Flip-
pant and Miss Spiteful--try by the methods suggested by their
names to make themselves attractive to Sir Charles. The
ladies criticize Miss Homely and are chagrined to learn that
she is the very lady whom Sir Charles has chosen for his fi-
ancée. He lectures the young ladies in a speech, the tenets
of which Rousseau's Sophie already knows:

> "You, ladies, rarely hear the voice of truth, and
> may, perhaps, frown at the unaccustomed sound.
> The greater part of you are nursed in folly and van-
> ity; . . . I speak the real sentiments of every rea-
> sonable man, when I tell you, that few of us ever
> think of taking a wife from among the gay things
> whom we follow at a ball." (56-57)

Sir Charles' friend, Mr. Steady, who has been present
during the above discussion, comments on the qualities of a
good wife. These qualities are quite similar to those of
Rousseau's Sophie. A good wife should be understanding,

124   <u>Emile</u> and Early Children's Literature

should possess a good temper and a degree of meekness,
should be discreet, should have a good name, and should be
neither foolish nor witty (58). In regard to her person, she
should be straight, clean, healthy, neither striking nor disa-
greeable (60). She should have a relish for books, a taste
for rational amusement, some fashionable accomplishments,
the "power of polishing the domestic scene," and a "pliancy
of disposition" (60-61). Rousseau did not oppose any of these
points, except for the relish for books, and he would agree
with the unstated moral: True beauty is internal, not external.

    The last selection in <u>The Juvenile Tatler</u> is "The Wary
Mother: A Drama." It shows virtually no influence by Rousseau since it deals with a subject which Rousseau never mentioned. The subject is stated beneath the title: "It is very
important for young women early to distrust men in general."
Rousseau did, however, mention that Sophie must be careful
to guard her honor and preserve a good reputation. Lady
Fenn is more specific in her giving of practical advice to
young ladies than Rousseau is or even than Dorothy Kilner is
in her work, <u>The Life and Perambulation of a Mouse.</u>

<u>The Life and Perambulation of a Mouse</u>

    Dorothy Kilner says she wrote <u>The Life and Perambu-</u>
<u>lation of a Mouse</u> "no less to instruct and improve, than . . .
to amuse and divert [the reader]."[20] The story has a frame:
during a cold winter when the author was visiting at Meadow
Hall, a young lady proposed for diversion that everyone present should tell his life's story. As the author tries to write
hers, she realizes how insipid it will be to the others. A
voice interrupts her: "Then write mine, which may be more
diverting" (264). Thus the mouse, Nimble, begins his tale,
but first the author interjects the following:

        But, before I proceed to relate my new little com-
        panion's history, I must beg leave to assure my
        readers, that, in earnest, I never heard a mouse
        speak in all my life; and only wrote the following
        narrative as being far more entertaining, and not
        less instructive, than my own life would have been.
        (265)

No doubt Rousseau would have objected to the use of an animal, just as the use of a fairy, to tell the story. Both the

Kilners, however, are as interested in entertaining as in-
structing; and their works follow Rousseau's to no appreci-
able degree.

Dorothy Kilner differs from Rousseau in her use of
admonition to warn children about cheating, lying and deceiv-
ing by giving an example of a girl who practiced those bad
habits and ended up by being transported for twenty-one
years, having narrowly escaped hanging (328). Another technique, that of the author's entering in her own person, giving
advice, and stating morals, is seen at the end of both Parts
I and II. At the end of Part I, she says: "I hope [my little
readers] have been wise enough to attend to the advice given
them in the preceding pages, although it was delivered to
them by one as insignificant as a MOUSE" (301). Part II
concludes with the following statement:

> And now I cannot take leave of all my little read-
> ers without once more begging them, for their own
> sakes, to endeavour to follow all the good advice
> the mouse has been giving them; and likewise warn-
> ing them to shun all those vices and follies, the
> practice of which renders children so contemptible
> and wicked. (334)

She also, as author, comments on one occasion on the reasons why not to fear noises in the dark (321).

There is no plot in this story. One critic says "the
abundance of incidents and the plentiful disasters compensate
for the lack of plot."[21] The events happen to the mouse
Nimble and his brothers, Longtail, Softdown, and Brighteyes.
In the course of their adventures, they overhear people in
the houses they invade in their pursuit of food. The reader
is to learn a lesson from these overheard conversations, as
well as from what happens to the mice. Dorothy Kilner
plainly states that the reader is to make the analogy from
the consequence of the mice not following their parent's advice (277). Rousseau was fond of analogy also, but never
used it in this way, applying the rules for a little creature
to children.

Most of the incidents involve either a mouse or a
child getting into trouble from not obeying or getting punished
for doing something wrong. Both the Kilner sisters do not
hesitate to impose death as a suitable punishment. For example, Softdown gets caught in a trap and is later killed be-

cause all the brothers did not follow their mother's parting
advice of not remaining in one house very long. Nimble says
of John's stepping on Softdown: "My very blood runs cold
within me at the recollection of seeing Softdown's blood as it
spirted from beneath the monster's foot; whilst the craunch
of his bones almost petrified me with horror" (276). And if
that were not enough, Brighteyes is tortured by being held
by his tail over the mouth of a cat. Miss Kilner, in her desire to preach against the wickedness of torturing helpless
animals, has the boy holding the mouse get surprised by his
father with the result that the boy gets a lecture and the poor
mouse drops right into the mouth of the cat (279). The remaining two mice have learned their lesson by experience,
the way Rousseau advocated; they leave that house.

There are also examples of crime and punishment involving the children in the story. For example, a young girl
was always frightened, for no reason of course, by dogs.
At tea one day, a dog comes in and heads for its mistress,
but the young lady is so excited she jumps up and overturns
the water-urn, and as Miss Kilner says, in part: "the hot
iron of which rolling out, set fire to her clothes, which in-
stantly blazed up, being only muslin, and burnt her arms,
face, and neck, most dreadfully" (267-68). This is punishment and severe punishment, but not of the kind Rousseau
advocated; that is, if the girl were burned because she
played with fire, her punishment would have been more in
keeping with her bad deed.

Most of Dorothy Kilner's characters are not developed
to any extent. Primarily they are puppets who perform to
learn a lesson. One child is interesting for his cleverness.
He is clever at playing tricks, as well as clever in his
schoolwork. This cleverness is consistent and unusual in
that a bad boy has a redeeming feature, although an adult
comments on the sad misuse of the boy's abilities (325).
The character of the mouse Nimble is interesting and if it
were created before Sarah Trimmer's Fabulous Histories
(1786), then it may be the first animal to tell a story of any
length from his own viewpoint. The general consensus of
opinion, however, seems to be that Fabulous Histories came
first. Miss Meigs remarks that Dorothy Kilner was inspired
by her friend Sarah Trimmer to write this story.[22] In either case, Rousseau would not want Emile to learn his lessons from mice instead of from a highly qualified teacher.

There are numerous subjects treated in this story

which are similar to those Rousseau advocated, but the list
of those in opposition to Rousseau's ideas is of equal length.
The former list consists of the attitude of kindness to, and
dependence on, servants (271, 307, 309), of kindness to animals (280), of no fear of the dark or noises in the dark
(319)--Rousseau felt children should play games in the dark
so they would not fear it--of contentment with one's station
in life (306, 310); and of the importance of virtue rather than
wealth (272, 285, 311). Examples of the last two will be
given in the discussion below of the Speedgo family. Dorothy
Kilner's attitude toward boarding schools is a disapproving
one in general. Rousseau favored individual tutoring over
schools also. Miss Kilner, however, recognizing that in
some cases, the children cannot remain at home, sees fit to
warn them about the tricks and wickedness of some children
in schools. Thus she is in opposition to Rousseau's negative
education--not exposing the child to vice. When Rousseau,
however, is ready for Emile to enter society, he begins to
warn him and reverses his idea of Emile's learning by experience. Thus the difference between Miss Kilner and Rousseau seems to be more a difference in opinion about the
proper age at which to warn the child, rather than about the
warning itself.

There is an example of an admirable, though poor,
woman, Betty Flood, who speaks of nursing a gentleman's
son (287). Since Miss Kilner so obviously approves of the
nurse, it is reasonable to conclude that she does not oppose
a mother giving out her child to a nurse. Rousseau's feelings were just the opposite. Miss Kilner does follow Rousseau in her idea of being prepared for any change in fortune;
however, she does so in her own way. A young servant girl,
Molly Mount, gets dismissed from her job because she is
honest enough to tell her young mistresses, the Speedgo sisters, that they are proud and contemptuous of their inferiors
(311). Sometime later, the Speedgo family loses its money,
the father dies, and the mother and girls are almost destitute; they cannot hold a servant's job long because they are
so ill-prepared for working. One sister, ill and hungry, appears by chance at the door of Molly Mount's farm; Molly,
always content with her own station in life, hardworking, and
virtuous is now the wife of a fairly prosperous farmer. Molly
takes the young lady in, cares for her, and learning who she
really is, sends for the girl's remaining family and gives
them a home. This story proves the virtuous will be happy
more than it proves that even the rich should be prepared
for a change in fortune; but the latter is implied. It is in-

teresting, however, that in Dorothy Kilner's next work, Anecdotes of a Boarding-School, which describes the education of
young girls, there is very little, if any, stress put upon what
these little ladies would do if their fathers lost their fortunes
or if they did not marry well.

Anecdotes of a Boarding-School

Dorothy Kilner's subtitle to Anecdotes of a Boarding-
School is An Antidote to the Vices of those Useful Seminaries.
This subtitle suggests the unfavorable attitude toward the
boarding school which was then prevalent. Miss Kilner believes that the evils of such a school counterbalance its advantages, and yet she states that it is necessary for the anonymous young lady to whom she addresses her book to attend
such a school since she lives a remote distance from a place
where she might gain instruction in the necessary polite accomplishments and since her mother has too many other children to tend to her education. Dr. Aikin was of the same
opinion; that is, there were a few reasons for boarding
schools to exist and for parents to send their children there;
however, both Dr. Aikin and Miss Kilner believed the mother
herself was the best governess, just as Rousseau believed.

The three-fold purpose for which Miss Kilner writes
is to protect the young lady from the evils of the boarding
school, to amuse her, and to instruct her. In regard to protection from the evils of boarding schools, Miss Kilner differs from Rousseau. She warns the young lady as a means
of protecting her innocence; this warning is in contrast to
Rousseau's idea of negative education, though, as I said in
the discussion of the preceding book, Rousseau also warns
Emile when the latter enters society. It is the difference in
age between Emile and Martha Beauchamp that is more significant.

Martha is between nine and ten years old when she
sets off for school. She has great incentive to learn, which
Rousseau felt was important, because her improvement determines her stay at school.[23] At school she gets teased,
lied to, and unjustly punished. Miss Kilner has the somewhat irritating habit of relating an incident, having Martha
write to her mother about the incident, and then having Mrs.
Beauchamp write back to Martha about the same incident.
Martha's teachers at school, her mother, and even her peer,
Miss Candid, serve as governesses to her. Martha's mother

and the headmistress, Mrs. Steward, come closest to following in the tradition of the all-wise tutor. Neither, however,
uses deceit as Emile's tutor does. Many of Martha's problems arise from the fact that some of the other teachers are
not as good or admirable as Mrs. Steward. In fact, the
worst teacher is Miss Starch, who is in charge of Martha's
age group. Martha accuses Miss Starch of laughing at bodily
infirmities and at people's dress (I, 78). Martha's mother
had warned about this kind of rudeness, as had Mary Wollstonecraft's Mrs. Mason.

In addition to learning from her various tutors, Martha learns from lectures sent to her in letters from her
mother (I, 85; II, 46) and those given to her in person by
Mrs. Steward. One of the longest episodes and without doubt
the longest lecture occurs when the girls (not Martha though)
are guilty of having their fortunes told by a gypsy (I, 99-
107). Martha never intentionally does anything wrong; she
knows superstition and belief in omens are wrong because her
father, on their way to boarding school, tells her a story
from which she learns that lesson (I, 26-39). She can thus
resist the gypsy. The gypsy episode concludes Volume I,
and the first one-third of Volume II is taken up by Mrs.
Steward's investigation, lecture, interpolated story of a similar incident with drastic consequences, and finally refusal to
punish the girls because they are sorrowful. The lecture
technique, the example, and the lack of punishment all differ
from Rousseau's tutor's actions on such an occasion. It is
interesting that the main reason the girls are not to have
their fortunes told is that believing in what a gypsy has to
say is believing that God made the gypsy His spokesman to
mankind, which He did not (II, 8); rather, Mrs. Steward explains that the happiness of the fortune told depends upon the
amount of money that the girl gives the gypsy (II, 13-14).

God and religion enter into the education of the girls
at school (I, 12, 17, 20, 57, 88-89; II, 7, 23, 43 and others). Dorothy Kilner includes the concept of the Eye that
sees everything (I, 15, 58), just as Mary Wollstonecraft and
Lady Fenn did. Various characters refer to the Bible, and
Martha's mother gives her a copy of it to take to school, a-
long with other books, including Mary Jane Kilner's The Adventures of a Pincushion and Memoirs of a Peg-Top (I, 20).
Martha astonishes her teacher with her reading ability (I, 71).
Thus Dorothy Kilner is in the same category as every other
writer considered here; she believes in the child's learning
to read at a much younger age than Rousseau did.

Miss Kilner discourages any belief in myth or in superstition; she includes a list of the gods and goddesses,
muses, graces, and others from mythology because a reading
of Gay's Fables brings up the question as to who the gods
were (II, 89-91). Mrs. Steward points out that these were
heathen gods and a knowledge of them is necessary for understanding poetry (II, 87). The teachers and even Mr. and Mrs.
Beauchamp speak against fancies of the imagination (I, 36),
superstition (I, 26), and fairies and giants (II, 24). In these
ideas, Miss Kilner agrees with Rousseau.

Dorothy Kilner also agrees with Rousseau on subjects
like punishment being suited to the crime. One example is
the punishment of extreme uneasiness of mind suiting the
crime of being superstitious (I, 38). Another similarity is
that both authors believe each child has an individual bent
which should be cultivated (I, 53). Both stress plain dress
(I, 60). Both believe in people setting a good example (I,
63). Both see the need for physical exercise (II, 80). Both
recognize evil in society (I, 66, 90; II, 34). Both have their
girls learn dancing and drawing (I, 75) and needlework (II,
40).

Rousseau and Dorothy Kilner differ in that Miss Kilner stresses not being a tattletale (I, 82, 89), a subject
Rousseau never mentions. She has her girls taught astronomy (II, 68), geography (II, 68, 76), history (II, 38, 81-82),
and writing (II, 38), subjects not domestic enough for Rousseau. These two authors differ in their attitude toward memorization. Miss Kilner seems inconsistent, for first she has
Martha object to evening prayers being said in French. Martha believes she must say hers in English since she does not
understand what she is saying in French (I, 72, 94-95).
Rousseau felt it was a mistake to learn another language at
an early age. Later Mrs. Steward has Martha and others
commit to memory certain short sentences about history or
geography, the purpose being that when they encounter the
character in history whom they have memorized a statement
about, it will make an impression on their minds and help
them to retain history better (II, 85).

Rousseau's effect on character and plot is slight; but
it is even less evident on the techniques the author uses for
teaching, as the above example shows. Mrs. Beauchamp in
a lecture claims that teaching by setting a good example is
better than teaching by offering advice (I, 91), but she seldom restricts herself to the former. On one occasion she

claims that Martha already knows how to behave in church
and thus does not need a lecture on the subject, but then she
lists all the things Martha does correctly (I, 21-22). One
unique technique, obviously different from Rousseau's, deserves mention. Miss Kilner lists the brief statements she
has Martha memorize (II, 67-70, 75-79, 80-84). The reader
is also expected to learn lessons from Dorothy Kilner's next
book, The Village School.

The Village School

Harvey Darton claims "The Village School was intended, among other things, to censure the vices of boarding
schools."[24] The children in the village of Rose Green attend
Mrs. Bell's school. When Harry Sturdy is very bad, the
children learn his parents have sent him away to a boarding
school.[25] There are many lessons to be learned as Darton
has said. The book is a difficult one to discuss because
there is no central character.[26] The teacher comes closest
to being a central character. The children who attend her
school all have names in the humours tradition, as do the
minor characters in the two works by Dorothy Kilner previously mentioned.

There is no perceptible influence on character by
Rousseau except perhaps in the fact that often the parent and
Mrs. Bell combine their efforts to correct a child. There
is some evidence, however, that Rousseau influenced the subjects treated, for The Village School attempts to teach kindness to animals (341, 382, 384-85) and the importance of
virtue rather than wealth (339, 342, 349).

Rousseau's idea of crime determining punishment is
vividly exemplified here. One child, Ralph Breakclod, the
protagonist of an interpolated story, actually dies because he
lies so much that his parents do not believe he is really ill
(371-78).[27] Another example of the crime-punishment idea
occurs when two little girls have their toys hung around their
necks all day for playing with them during school time. After school, their toys are confiscated (336-37).

At the same time that Miss Kilner doles out these
punishments, she institutes an elaborate system of rewards,
quite contrary to Rousseau's teachings. The children often
receive books and cakes for rewards (339, 383, 392). As
punishment they go without supper (342), spend the night at

school (341), or sit tied to their chairs during school (349);
also they may get whipped (345, 353).

In addition to the idea of crime befitting the punishment, Rousseau's effect on plot is evident in the use of interpolated stories for the purpose of teaching a lesson for
that particular situation. There are a number of them (339,
350, 358, 360, 371, 386). They cover the usual subjects that
children are to learn. The last one listed (386) is worth no-
ting. It is the story of two dogs: a handsome one, Cato,
and an ugly one, Syphax. Cato gets many privileges because
he is handsome; Syphax, his brother, does not. Twice Syphax
saves his master's life, while Cato merely plays nearby.
For a reward Syphax gets taken into the house, and Cato gets
sent outside where he does not fare well because he is so
spoiled and unkind. He dies not long afterwards. When the
clergyman, Mr. Right, relates this story, he has to explain
to Roger Riot that it has an analogy with humans (389).
Rousseau was also fond of analogy. Roger Riot is difficult
to teach, however, for prior to this occasion, he pushed a
small child down a well, where the little boy drowned (363).
This fact is mentioned to point out the unusual number of
deaths in this story, the final one being truly unique in the
annals of children's literature.

The Village School closes with an episode in which
Mrs. Bell takes in a poor lady with a sprained ankle. She
has been following her son on his way to be hanged, and she
says to the schoolchildren:

> "When he was a child at school he never took any
> delight in his learning, but used to saunter away
> his time and be idle; and, all I could say to him,
> I never could persuade him to be diligent, and so
> he got into bad company, . . . and so he went
> from one fault to another till at last he commited
> that for which he is now going to suffer." (401)

Mrs. Bell comforts the poor woman after she lectures the
school children in the above manner, so contrary to Rousseau's. The woman goes to bed; Mrs. Bell stays up and
sews by candlelight a shirt for a neighbor. The house some-
how catches on fire and burns to the ground. This is the
fate of the good and diligent Mrs. Bell:

> Some bones were the next day found in the rubbish,
> but the flesh was so entirely consumed as to make

> it impossible to distinguish Mrs. Bell from the
> poor woman she so charitably assisted. (402)

The final sentence is a comment about being careful with
candles.

     This unique ending is absolutely in opposition to Rous-
seau's ideas of punishment. It seems too severe to be included merely to teach the child to be careful with candles.
Miss Kilner destroys the good example she set up in the
character of Mrs. Bell by having her be so careless. One
critic says Mrs. Bell's death is the result of Miss Kilner's
inability to contrive any other way of finishing her story. [28]
It would be comforting to think that, and it would be more in
keeping with Rousseau's ideas. Rousseau, of course, never
mentioned death to Emile at all. In contrast to Dorothy Kilner is her sister, whose stories are lighter in tone; Mary
Jane Kilner includes the death of a dog, Hector, in Jemima
Placid, but that is the only death recorded in the three works
by her being considered here, the first of which is Jemima
Placid.

Jemima Placid

     Mary Jane Kilner's Jemima Placid has been dated
1788. Her other works, The Adventures of a Pincushion and
Memoirs of a Peg-Top, appear to have been written earlier,
for they were published in America by 1788 by Isaiah Thomas. E. V. Lucas dates Jemima Placid about 1785, but at
the same time he does not know who the author is. In his
"Preface," Lucas quotes the original preface which sets forth
the purpose of the author:

> "The main design of this publication is to prove
> from example that pain of disappointment will be
> much increased by ill-temper, and that to yield to
> the force of necessity will be found wiser than vain-
> ly to oppose it. The contrast between the princi-
> pal character with the peevishness of her cousins'
> temper is intended as an incitement of that placid
> disposition which will form the happiness of social
> life in every stage."[29]

The subtitle, The Advantages of Good-Nature, suggests that
it is advantageous to be good. Mary Jane Kilner, like her
sister Dorothy and so many other writers of the period, con-

trasts two kinds of behavior--Jemima's and that of her cousins. Rousseau would not have Jemima witness the naughty
tricks and fighting of the cousins that Miss Kilner has her
see. In fact, Florence Barry sees none of Rousseau's ideas
in Jemima Placid. She says: "A Rousseauist might have
overlooked the philosophy in this little book, . . . for there
is not an ounce of theory in it."[30] It is true that Jemima
Placid is more in the tradition of Anecdotes of a Boarding-
School than in the tradition of Emile.[31]

      The author admonishes (226), lectures (256, 258), and
gives examples (249) in order to teach her readers how to
behave. The subjects Miss Kilner treats are sometimes
those which Rousseau felt were important, such as kindness
to animals (239-40), limited indulgence (234), sewing (254),
plain dress (236-37), moderate eating (237), different rules
for boys and girls (245), role of the father in his son's education (251), and most interestingly, unnecessary fear of insects (248-49). Rousseau said the child reared in a house
free from spiders would fear spiders; consequently, he wanted the child's nurse to show him, at a young age, carefully
selected things, such as insects, so he would learn there is
no reason to fear.

      Mary Jane Kilner's views contrast with Rousseau's in
that she does not advocate the mother nursing her own child.
Miss Kilner's technique differs from Rousseau's in that she,
like her sister, sprinkles her works with practical jokes.
In this story, there is an example of a child putting pepper
in a snuff box (247-48).

      In the idea of being content with one's own sex, this
author has expressed a view which could probably be called
a variation of Rousseau's idea of being content with one's
station in life. Miss Kilner also has a variation of Rousseau's crime-punishment idea in an interpolated story about
the friendly spur (252-53). A conscientious tutor applies the
spur to whatever part of the child misbehaves; that is, if the
little girl droops her head, the friendly spur taps her on the
back of the neck; if the little boy puts his arms on the table
at dinner time, the spur touches his elbows (253).

      In Jemima Placid, as in The Adventures of a Pin-
cushion and in Memoirs of a Peg-Top, Mary Jane Kilner presents few topics, if any, that have not been discussed by other writers. Even when she does treat subjects Rousseau
felt strongly about, they are not so clearly attributable to

Rousseau as to enable one to say she was a disciple of Rousseau.

The Adventures of a Pincushion

The purpose of The Adventures of a Pincushion, perhaps Miss Kilner's earliest book of the three discussed here, is, in its author's words "to avoid exciting any wrong impression, and, by sometimes blending instruction with amusement, to make it the more easily retained."[32] And further, the author's motive is "that of presenting the juvenile reader with a few pages which should be innocent of corrupting, if they did not amuse" (viii).[33]

The overall plan of the book is for a pincushion to change hands, and while in each little girl's possession, it overhears and witnesses incidents, some of which it finds necessary to comment on. A critic compares the pincushion to a chorus character who objects and comments on the action, but does not take part in it.[34]

The story opens with two sisters who are complete opposites in both actions and appearance. Martha, the good girl, is pitted by smallpox; Charlotte, the bad one, is quite attractive--on the outside anyway (18). Martha, in putting her time to good use, makes the pincushion; and thereafter its adventures begin.

Rousseau's opposition to fables and fairies was clear. Miss Kilner, therefore, felt it necessary to explain to Rousseau and others of the school which opposed the fabulous, as well as to her young readers, what they can assume about a pincushion that talks:

> Perhaps you never thought that such things as are
> inanimate, could be sensible of any thing which
> happens, as they can neither hear, see, or under-
> stand; and as I would not willingly mislead your
> judgment. I would, previous to your reading
> this work, inform you that it is to be understood
> as an imaginary tale, in the same manner as when
> you are at play, you sometimes call yourselves
> gentlemen, and ladies, though you know you are
> only little boys, or girls. So, when you read of
> birds and beasts speaking and thinking, you know
> it is not so in reality, any more than your amuse-

ments, which you frequently call making believe.
(13)

I have included this lengthy quote because it adequately sums
up the feelings of Miss Kilner, Sarah Trimmer, and others--
all of whom obviously opposed Rousseau in this area of fic-
tion.

Rousseau's influence on the whole book is slight. The
characters are personifications of various traits; the plot is
haphazard and somewhat contrived in spite of the author's
attempts to the contrary. The subjects treated, however,
show the author has some of the same interests that Rousseau had.

Rousseau stressed a kindly attitude toward servants,
and he criticized vain young girls for taking too long to dress.
Miss Kilner is concerned with the treatment of servants and
with promptness in dressing, but with a slightly different emphasis. Charlotte takes too long to dress because she needs
help; and after having insulted her maid, she has to dress
herself (21). Thus her lack of promptness in dressing is
not the result of vanity, but of rudeness. Miss Kilner, like
Rousseau, wants her readers to learn contentment with their
position in life, for the pincushion tells them that while it
was imprisoned under a dresser, its fuming and fretting did
not help at all (59). In Part II, one of the admirable characters, Hannah, is in the tradition of Sophie, for she wears
no ornaments, but dresses neatly (88).

There is some contrast with Rousseau's ideas in the
children's competition with one another, as in a spelling bee,
about which Miss Kilner says: "A precedency in the ring was
coveted with great ardour, and encouraged a spirit of emula-
tion among [the children], as to stand first . . . was regarded as an acknowledgement of superior excellence" (73).
Of course, Emile used to race other little boys for cakes;
however, Rousseau's approval of competition in physical
sports does not necessarily mean he would encourage competition in intellectual sports. The little girls learn geography,
history, and writing. They write to help them retain (51-52).
Rousseau believed that the education of girls should be restricted to lessons of a domestic nature.

Miss Kilner moralizes on occasion as, for example,
at the conclusion of the book when the pincushion remarks on
the folly of taking pride in those possessions and distinctions

which it says are "precarious in enjoyment and uncertain in
possession" (104). The author also includes an interpolated
story which is in the tradition of the Ralph Breakclod story
mentioned in the discussion of The Village School. Mary
Jane Kilner, possessed of a little more compassion than her
sister, has Betsey Lloyd merely crippled for life, not die as
Ralph does. When Betsey is late getting home, she says a
horse has frightened her (47). Her lie goes undetected, but
later she does get frightened by a horse, and she breaks her
leg. Thereafter she is a cripple--a punishment in the tradition of Rousseau's idea of punishment. Yet there is little
influence by Rousseau on the whole, although the authors do
have some ideas in common. Mary Jane Kilner's next work,
Memoirs of a Peg-Top is also only slightly affected by Rousseau's Emile.

Memoirs of a Peg-Top

As The Adventures of a Pincushion met with success,
Miss Kilner decided to try her hand at a similar book for
boys. Memoirs of a Peg-Top was also written to amuse and
instruct. Miss Kilner makes the interesting point that although justice and truth are laws for both sexes, she believes
her readers are more likely to approve and accept these
laws if they are written in a manner especially interesting
to readers of that sex. [35]

Memoirs of a Peg-Top is the story of a top that has
some adventures and witnesses others about which it comments to its audience. It often moralizes; for example,
when one boy is bad and brags about his deeds, he is overheard and punished. The top says:

> And indeed I have often had occasion to remark in
> the scenes in which I have been engaged, that how-
> ever vice may triumph for a time, it is generally
> discovered in the end, and meets with its deserved
> retribution. (29)

Generally the bad boy gets punished; then the top comments
to reinforce the lesson. This procedure is not in keeping
with Rousseau's ideas about teaching.

There is a story of a greedy boy, Tom Swallowell
(30-37), who supposedly learns not to be greedy because another boy mixes cow dung with the custard Tom wants and

begins to eat while blindfolded. There is another quite
lengthy crime-punishment story in which Rousseau would have
delighted. George Mealwell works for Mr. Bakeall, the ba-
ker. Supposedly making deliveries, George finds the top and
challenges Charles Heedmore to a game. The horse, with
its cart full of bakery items, gets frightened and runs off,
destroying the cart in the process. George decides to lie to
his employer and tell him that he was hurt in the accident.
He then knocks his shoulder against a post in order to bruise
himself, and he takes a briar and scratches around his eye
to make that look bad. The appropriate punishment is that
he gets a thorn from the briar in his eye. In pain he goes
to his employer, and the truth comes out; Mr. Bakeall plans
to increase the bruise on George's shoulder (58-82).

There are other lessons taught on subjects such as
not fighting (39), not laughing at the suffering of others (104),
not doing lessons on time (43), and on other subjects necessary to the education of a boy reared with other boys, but
not reared in isolation as Emile was.

There is no single tutor-figure in this book or in The
Adventures of a Pincushion. The characters again are named
in the humours tradition. Rousseau does not appear to have
influenced Mary Jane Kilner to any extent. In a comparison
between the Kilner sisters' works and those of Thomas Day
and Maria Edgeworth, for example, Rousseau's influence
seems truly slight on the former. It is even less perceptible
in the writings of the two authors who shall be discussed in
the next chapter, Hannah More and Sarah Trimmer.

Notes

1.   Cornelia Lynde Meigs, "Roots in the Past up to 1840,"
      A Critical History of Children's Literature: A Sur-
      vey of Children's Books in English from Earliest
      Times to the Present, Prepared in 4 pts. , ed. Cor-
      nelia L. Meigs (New York: Macmillan, 1953), p. 94.

2.   Gillian Elise Avery, Nineteenth Century Children: He-
      roes and Heroines in English Children's Stories,
      1780-1900 (London: Hodder and Stoughton, 1965),
      p. 234. F. J. Harvey Darton, Children's Books in
      England: Five Centuries of Social Life (Cambridge
      at the University Press, 1932), p. 168, dates Cob-
      webs (1783?), Tatler (1783?), and Spectator (1789).

He makes no mention of the Fables.

3. Darton, p. 164, and Florence Valentine Barry, A Century of Children's Books (New York: George H. Doran Co. , 1923), p. 128, are two.

4. John Mackay Shaw, Childhood in Poetry: A Catalogue (5 vols.; Detroit: Gale Research Co. , 1967), III, 1446; Percival Horace Muir, English Children's Books, 1600-1900 (New York: Praeger, 1954), p. 94, suggests both possibilities.

5. Mary Wollstonecraft, Thoughts on the Education of Daughters (London: Printed for J. Johnson, 1787), p. 16, is one who mentions The Life and Perambulation of a Mouse by Dorothy Kilner.

6. As mentioned previously, use has been made of the British Museum Catalogue's distinction between the Kilners' works. Most critics agree with this distinction.

7. Darton, p. 167, mentions Solomon Lovechild, but he does not appear in the three books under discussion here.

8. Ibid. , p. 168.

9. Avery, p. 15.

10. [Lady Eleanor Fenn], Cobwebs to Catch Flies: or, Dialogues in Short Sentences, Adapted to Children from the Age of Three to Eight Years (2 vols.; London: Lockwood and Co. , n.d.), I, 22. This edition has been dated by a librarian at Harvard as 1871(?). It is obviously a nineteenth-century edition. Hereafter any reference to this work will be indicated by the volume numbers and page numbers in parentheses in the body of the text.

11. See page 109 above.

12. See page 19 above.

13. See Chapter II above.

14. Mrs. Teachwell and Her Family [Lady Eleanor Fenn],

The Fairy Spectator: or The Invisible Monitor (London: Printed by and for John Marshall, 1790), p. 16. All future references to this book will be indicated by the page numbers in parentheses in the body of the text.

15. It is interesting to note that Miss Sprightly first dreamed about the fairy after having read from Gay's Fables and from a book called The Mother, Nurse, and Fairy.

16. See Chapter II above.

17. A Society of Young Ladies Under the Tuition of Mrs. Teachwell [Lady Eleanor Fenn], The Juvenile Tatler (London: Printed and Sold by J. Marshall and Co., 1789), vi-vii. All future references to this book will be indicated by the page numbers in parentheses in the body of the text.

18. See the "wall of brass" speech, page 18 above

19. Barry, p. 119. On p. 119-20, she includes a summary of the "Innocent Romp."

20. M. P. [Dorothy Kilner], "To the Reader," The Life and Perambulation of a Mouse (London: Printed for John Harris, 1828). Hereafter the edition used will be the one found in A Storehouse of Stories, ed. Charlotte M. Yonge (1st series; London: Macmillan, 1872), p. 262-334. All future references to it will be indicated by the page numbers in parentheses in the body of the text.

21. Avery, p. 30.

22. Meigs, p. 92.

23. M. P. [Dorothy Kilner], Anecdotes of a Boarding-School: or An Antidote to the Vices of those Useful Seminaries (2 vols.; London: Printed and Sold by John Marshall, [1790]), I, 23. All future references to this work will be indicated by the volume numbers and page numbers in parentheses in the body of the text.

24. Darton, p. 165.

25. Dorothy Kilner, The Village School, in A Storehouse of
    Stories, ed. Charlotte M. Yonge (1st series; Lon-
    don: Macmillan, 1872), p. 371. All future refer-
    ences to this work will be indicated by the page
    numbers in parentheses in the body of the text.

26. Muir, p. 83, calls Jacob Steadfast the central charac-
    ter, but he is not mentioned until midway in the
    book.

27. This is obviously a variation of Aesop's fable of the
    boy who cried "Wolf."

28. Avery, p. 30.

29. Forgotten Tales of Long Ago, selected by E. V. Lucas
    (London: Wells, Gardner, Darton and Co., 1906),
    p. vii. The copy of Jemima Placid which shall be
    used hereafter does not have this preface included;
    it is Jemima Placid, in A Storehouse of Stories, ed.
    Charlotte M. Yonge (1st series; London: Macmil-
    lan, 1872), p. 223-62. Future references will be
    indicated by page numbers in parentheses.

30. Barry, p. 129.

31. Jemima Placid and Martha Beauchamp are the only two
    extremely sentimental children in all the stories
    covered in this paper. The name of Martha's moth-
    er is Jemima. Jemima receives a message from
    a Mr. Steward; Mrs. Steward is Martha's teacher.
    Both books rely on the use of letters. In both cases
    the mother cannot care for her daughter and sends
    her off where she is exposed to others who are
    naughty and bad.

32. [Mary Jane Kilner], The Adventures of a Pincushion:
    Designed Chiefly for the Uses of Young Ladies
    (Worcester, Mass.: Isaiah Thomas, 1788), p. vi.
    All future references to this work will be indicated
    by the page numbers in parentheses in the body of
    the text.

33. The italics which Miss Kilner used for this entire sen-
    tence have been omitted.

34. Meigs, p. 93.

35. [Mary Jane Kilner], Memoirs of a Peg-Top (Worcester, Mass.: Isaiah Thomas, 1788), p. 8. All future references to this work will be indicated by the page numbers in parentheses in the body of the text.

Chapter VII

Hannah More and Sarah Kirby Trimmer

Both Hannah More and Sarah Trimmer were aware of
Rousseau's views on education; however, there is some doubt
as to when they learned about those views. Hannah More
disagreed with Rousseau in her Strictures on the Modern
System of Female Education (1801), but this book was written
after her Cheap Repository Tracts (1795-1798), the work
which is of concern to students of the history of children's
literature. Mrs. Trimmer disagreed with Rousseau in her
periodical The Guardian of Education (1802-1806); her children's books were written earlier--An Easy Introduction to
the Knowledge of Nature (1780) and Fabulous Histories (1786),
later called The History of the Robins.[1] I believe that Miss
More knew of Rousseau before writing her Cheap Repository
Tracts and that she chose to ignore his ideas; Mrs. Trimmer, on the other hand, followed some of Rousseau's ideas,
suggesting that she knew his views, but did not reject them
until a number of years later. She does not, however, owe
a large debt to Rousseau.

Hannah More lived a long and full life well into the
nineteenth century. She lived with her four sisters--none of
the five ever married--and she survived them all. It is difficult to believe that the little lady of eighty-eight, who died
in 1833, was the same gay, charming creature whom David
Garrick called "Nine" because he felt all nine muses were
combined in her. In the late 1780's Hannah More, friend of
Dr. Johnson, Mrs. Montague, Horace Walpole, the Wartons,
Joshua Reynolds and other famous people, became interested
in the Sunday School Movement. It was this interest that
eventually led her to write a preface condemning drama and
attach it to her own successful plays when they were being
republished. As she became more pious, and also as the
result of the death of her very dear friend, David Garrick,
she gave up London society. Of course, in addition to Garrick, many of her other famous friends had died by this
time. Her interest in religion also led her to write the
Cheap Repository Tracts (1795-1798), following her success-

ful <u>Village Politics</u> (1792), written, in the words of one critic, "to counteract the teachings of Tom Paine and the French
Revolution."[2] She proved she knew how to reach the minds
and hearts of the poor by her success with <u>Village Politics</u>,
and it was at the poor that the Sunday School Movement was
aimed.

        Robert Raikes of Gloucester was the first to get the
Sunday School Movement underway. According to one critic,
the dirty children playing in the streets on Sunday morning
so appalled Mr. Raikes that he resolved that even children
of factory workers should learn reading, writing, cleanli-
ness, and religion.[3] Hannah More and her sisters set up a
school in Cheddar for the same purpose. They contributed
money, sought a teacher, and explained the purpose to neighborhood people; Miss More even wrote some textbooks.
Eventually she was instrumental in opening a Cheddar School
of Industry--a trade school--and there were attempts to
draw the parents of the children to the schools to learn reading and religion. Hannah More wrote her <u>Cheap Repository</u>
<u>Tracts</u> for this poor, mostly illiterate, class of adults to
have some moral tales to read. She did not write them for
children, but as the poor children had little else they could
afford to buy to read, they read these tracts also.[4] Charlotte Yonge says their simplicity and interest make them appeal to children.[5] Another factor is their religious nature
makes it unlikely that they would contain anything unsuitable
for children.

        By 1795, the date of the first published <u>Tract</u>, the
French Revolution was over. Hannah More was unsympathet-
ic toward that cause and always maintained an active dislike
of the French. It is entirely possible that she had read
Rousseau's works, which contributed to the Revolution, without necessarily liking or agreeing with Rousseau. By 1801
when her <u>Strictures on the Modern System of Female Educa-</u>
<u>tion</u> was published, she had read Rousseau, for she says:

                Many authors will more infallibly complete the ruin
                of the loose and ill-disposed: but perhaps there
                never was a net of such exquisite art, and inex-
                tricable workmanship, spread to entangle innocence,
                and ensnare inexperience, as the writings of Rous-
                seau; and, unhappily, the victim does not even
                struggle in the toils, because part of the delusion
                consists in his imagining that he is set at liberty.[6]

Miss More is not usually specific, although she is when she states her opposition to Rousseau's idea of delaying religious education for the child (352). She is not as far from Rousseau's beliefs as she may have thought, however, when she says:

> When a man of sense comes to marry, it is a companion whom he wants, and not an artist. It is not merely a creature who can paint, and play, and sing, and draw, and dress, and dance; it is a being who can comfort and counsel him; one who can reason, and reflect and feel and judge, and discourse and discriminate, one who can assist him in his affairs, lighten his cares, sooth his sorrows, purify his joys, strengthen his principles, and educate his children. (329)

Almost twenty years prior to her Strictures, Miss More wrote Sacred Dramas especially for children. She took such Biblical stories as Moses in the Bulrushes and David and Goliath and tried her best to remain faithful to the Biblical account. She succeeded so admirably in her intention that there is no reason to discuss any possible influence by Rousseau; any similarities which might be present would not result from a conscious effort to follow Rousseau's ideas. Rousseau's influence, if present in Miss More's fictional writings considered here, would be in her Cheap Repository Tracts.

Cheap Repository Tracts

Hannah More's Tracts enjoyed an unusual popularity--over two million were sold within the first year. None was more popular, more well known, or even more typical than "The Shepherd of Salisbury Plain."[7] This tale shows its author's opposition to Rousseau on a few points and her concern generally with topics and ideas that Rousseau did not mention. She states her purpose in the "Advertisement" to the Tracts as "not only to counteract vice and profligacy on the one hand, but error, discontent and false religion on the other" (190).

The shepherd is one of the two main characters; the other is Mr. Johnson, a gentleman, who meets the shepherd in traveling across the plains of Wiltshire. Mr. Johnson is a man who admires the works of God in nature and who

seeks to help those who are true Christians. The shepherd
is such a Christian; he is also a neatly but plainly dressed
man who is content with his station in life. Rousseau would
have admired those qualities in a man. The shepherd over-
sees his children's education, such as it is; and he encourages each one to do some work for the good of all. Rousseau would have approved of everyone in the shepherd's family being industrious.

   The plot of the story is very simple. Mr. Johnson
meets the shepherd, puts him to various tests--all of which
the shepherd passes, and rewards him with a larger house.
Mr. Johnson is also instrumental in getting the shepherd the
job of parish clerk and Mary, the shepherd's wife, a small
school for girls. The plot shows no influence by Rousseau
unless it be negative influence.

   The subjects treated by Miss More show little similarity to Rousseau's ideas. The shepherd pays off his debts
(196); Mr. Johnson learns a lesson in thrift from the shepherd (193, 195). Rousseau, however, never mentions debts
or thrift. The shepherd teaches his children to read from
the Bible (192); whereas Rousseau opposed children's being
exposed to religion at an early age. The shepherd claims
that he needs God's grace to help him withstand evil thoughts
(199). Rousseau did not believe in original sin, and the idea
that the shepherd is tempted to think evil thoughts out in the
fields alone is contrary to Rousseau's idea that isolation prevents evil from entering the heart.

   In the testing of the shepherd, Hannah More employs
a technique used by the fairy in Lady Fenn's The Fairy Spectator. Mr. Johnson visits the shepherd on Sunday; he
learns that the shepherd's family are always on time for
church, that they will not go for ale on Sunday, and that
they maintain the Sabbath in an appropriate manner. The
passing of these tests is the basis for a reward; Rousseau,
of course, did not approve of rewards.

   In the praise of simple taste in food and clothing and
in neatness in dress and at home (196), Hannah More agrees
with Rousseau. In the idea of children helping and working
in little ways (193) and in the idea of the girls learning knit-
ting, sewing, and spinning (200), the two authors also agree;
but these ideas are not uniquely Rousseau's.

   Hannah More uses examples, lectures, and even pro-

paganda techniques. Seldom, if ever, does she use learning
by experience, Rousseau's method. She uses propaganda to
help convince the poor that they should be content with their
station in life. The shepherd says to Mr. Johnson:

> I wonder all working men do not derive as great
> joy and delight as I do from thinking how God has
> honoured poverty! Oh! sir, what great, or rich,
> or mighty men have had such honour put on them,
> or their condition, as shepherds, tentmakers, fish-
> ermen, and carpenters have had? (192)

Whether or not the poor people were more content with their
poverty after reading the Tracts is not known, but they certainly did buy them and read them. Sarah Trimmer's works
were not so popular, perhaps because they were more ex-
pensive,[8] perhaps because they did not appeal to the poor as
much. Sarah Trimmer's children's books, however, were
quite popular in spite of Muir's statement that "she was a
writer about children, rather than for them. Her main concern was to instill into parents a knowledge of what she conceived to be the true principles of moral upbringing."[9]

An Easy Introduction to the Knowledge of Nature

Sarah Kirby Trimmer, mother of twelve children,
naturally had an interest in education. Like Hannah More,
she had an interest in the Sunday School Movement, helping
set up a school at Brentford and even writing a book on the
promotion and management of Sunday schools. She also became very pious and eventually quite outspoken against Rousseau. Mrs. Trimmer spoke against fairy tales and against
Rousseau's ideas on education in her Guardian of Education
(1802-1806) which a critic has called "a periodical to criticise
and examine books for children and books on education, so
that only good ones might spread abroad."[10] Her work on
the periodical came much later than her writings for chil-
dren--An Easy Introduction to the Knowledge of Nature (1780)
and The History of the Robins (1786).

Someone suggested to Mrs. Trimmer that she might
carry on the tradition of Mrs. Barbauld's Lessons for Children. She did just that in her Easy Introduction to the Knowledge of Nature. One critic says that the book is:

> a set of conversational lessons on the same plan

> [as Mrs. Barbauld's], written with less skill and
> grace, and more of that insidious sense of patron-
> age which creeps into even the most wholehearted
> of educational efforts.[11]

Indeed Mrs. Trimmer seems to have lifted subjects and descriptions from Lessons for Children. At the same time,
another critic makes the point that Mrs. Trimmer may have
been inspired by Buffon, who also inspired Rousseau.[12] The
interest in natural history is obvious in both Mrs. Trimmer's
and Rousseau's books. The critics are agreed that An Easy
Introduction shows the influence of Rousseau; one critic calls
the influence "apparent";[13] another says Mrs. Trimmer's im-
pulse probably "came far more than she knew from Rousseau."[14]

Mrs. Trimmer's narrator states her purpose is to instruct and amuse.[15] At the beginning of Part III, the unnamed governess[16] asks the children, Charlotte and Henry,
if they have not "really found the amusement and instruction"
that she promised them (141).

In one way, the all-wise, ever-present governess is
just what Rousseau advocated for Emile; she takes the children for walks so they can see the elements of nature and
God's creatures for themselves. She generally allows the
children to discover something; then she names it and describes its uses. This emphasis on use is in keeping with
Rousseau's doctrine. In the absence of the actual object,
such as a camel, she teaches by pictures (62). She also
uses analogy. Surely Rousseau would have appreciated her
analogy of the earth's revolving around the sun being like a
spit with a fowl on it revolving above the fire, not the fire
going around the immovable spit (122).

The governess is unlike Emile's tutor, however, in
that her principal teaching technique is lecturing. The children supposedly ask questions, but the book is a monologue.
For this reason, the children are not developed as characters at all. The governess states morals and maxims. For
example, she says: "Let it be a rule never to waste what
such numbers would be glad to have" (27). She also lists
vegetables and flowers. Listing is less likely to make an
impression on the child's mind than actually seeing each vegetable and flower would. No doubt, Rousseau would not approve of lists, for children cannot gain experience that way.
One other characteristic of the governess contrasts her with

Emile's tutor. She seems to give Henry the idea of gluttony
when they enter the fruit orchard, for she says, in part:

> Do you not wish they were all ripe, Henry? Then
> what excellent tarts we could make! And what
> feasts we should have! Well, have a little patience,
> my dear; they will soon be ripe; and then you
> shall have plenty. (31)

Rousseau may have had some effect on the plot; that
is, there is no plot, only a series of episodes contrived by
the governess in order for the children to see and learn a-
bout nature. Emile's tutor worked in just the same way.
There are about four interpolated stories (22, 31-32, 52-53),
which the governess tells to emphasize her point. Most
show Rousseau's idea of punishment suiting the crime, although they are to teach lessons about impatience and greed.
One story on greed concerns a little boy who eats green
gooseberries and currants. He becomes sick and pale; he
gets worms in his bowels from eating the green fruit. His
punishment is not as drastic as the worm description might
lead the reader to believe. He simply does not get well until after all the fruit is ripe and eaten by the other children.
The governess says, "Was he not rightly punished for being
so undutiful and greedy" (32).

There are a number of subjects similar to those
Rousseau taught, but they are not always treated in the same
way. The love of nature with a knowledge of plants and animals is the main theme of Mrs. Trimmer's book; yet she,
like Mrs. Barbauld, gives God credit for all. Like Mrs.
Barbauld, she teaches the children about metals, ores, and
gems, and about the seasons of the year; about the life of a
caterpillar, as well as about all kinds of animals--both domestic and wild. Mrs. Barbauld, writing for the younger
child, restricted herself to domestic animals. Kindness to
animals is emphasized by the catalogue of animals cited
(54, 56, 76, 84). Mrs. Trimmer includes, as part of kindness to animals, refraining from angling; she feels angling
is a cruel sport (93), as is cock-fighting (67).

Geography and astronomy make up part of the children's lessons (90-95, 133, 134-40). In general, Mrs.
Trimmer includes more information on the subjects she
treats than does either Mrs. Barbauld or Rousseau. For
example, from the geography lesson, she tries to give the
children a knowledge of the sea (96-99), how to cross it,

how ships sail, how the captain uses a compass, the importance of trade winds, and the value of maps (109-17). In
her extensive descriptions of trees and flowers, she seems
to have influenced John Aikin. The idea of knowledge for
its own sake, however, would not coincide with Rousseau's
belief that knowledge should be useful.

Specifically, Mrs. Trimmer follows Rousseau's ideas
in her emphasis on exercise (8, 57), unnecessary fear of
spiders (79), and dislike of ornaments (104). The reason
she gives for the last point is interesting. She claims gems
and gold and silver "come out of the bowels of the earth" and
silks are "from the entrails of a little crawling worm" (105).
She does not maintain that every boy should learn a trade in
case Fortune is not kind to him; rather, she says the rich
should "learn to behave with kindness and condescension" to
the poor. It is to the poor that the rich owe their shoes,
houses, ploughed fields, sheared sheep, and many other
things (105).

Mrs. Trimmer encourages her children to read about
the things that they discuss (36, 81, 109). Mrs. Trimmer
also opposes Rousseau in the third part of her book where
she discusses mankind, the Bible, and God. Her description
of mankind consists mainly of telling about his soul (142-46).
She describes God (147-49), and she offers to convince the
children that "there is a God by the Works of Creation" (149).
She does this by pointing out that jewels come from the
earth, the silk from a worm, and God made both the earth
and the worm (154). She gives numerous other examples
(155-58), drawing each from the book of nature and attributing each to God. She encourages Charlotte to study the book
of nature, but to remember another book displays the goodness of God even more wonderfully--the Bible. Rousseau,
in the Savoyard Vicar section of Emile, said close the Bible
and open the book of nature.[17]

Mrs. Trimmer does not close the Bible; in fact, she
tells the children that the next day they will begin the Old
Testament. She will explain what they do not understand,
and she trusts "it will please God, of his infinite goodness,
to open your minds to understand the Scripture" (166). Thus
she ends her book with a statement directly contrary to Rousseau's belief. Her next book, however, is less contrary to
Rousseau's beliefs.

The History of the Robins

By far Mrs. Trimmer's most popular book, The History of the Robins was reprinted until at least the 1870's and was, according to one critic, very influential for a hundred years.[18] The book is especially noteworthy for its point of view; that is, much of the story is written from the point of view of a family of robin redbreasts. Dicky, one of the baby birds, gives the following description:

> a great round red face appeared before the nest
> with a pair of enormous staring eyes, a very large
> beak, and below that a wide mouth, with two rows
> of bones, that looked as if they could grind us all
> to pieces in an instant. About the top of this
> round face, and down the sides, hung something
> black, but not like feathers.[19]

Dicky is describing the gardener at the Benson home.[20] Since Rousseau disapproved of fairy tales, he would disapprove of telling a story from this point of view, but Mrs. Trimmer, like Dorothy Kilner, hopes to quiet the opposition by having the readers learn from the birds, as well as from the children in the story. Her primary objective is to show children how to behave toward animals. She says in the "Advertisement" that she hopes

> that the mode of conveying instruction on this sub-
> ject, which the author of the following sheets has
> adopted will engage the attention of young minds,
> and prove instrumental to the happiness of many an
> innocent animal.

In her conclusion, Mrs. Trimmer restates this purpose, and at the same time she tells something about her teaching techniques, techniques which Rousseau would approve of, for the most part: "From the foregoing examples, I hope my young readers will select the best for their own imitation, and take warning by the rest, otherwise my histories are written in vain" (213). Rousseau permitted teaching by examples, if the examples were admirable; but he rejected showing bad children or bad deeds. Mrs. Trimmer uses analogy, which Rousseau also used, but not in the same way; that is, Mrs. Trimmer turns a bird's always eating moderately into a lesson for little boys to do the same (35), and she makes an analogy between bees gathering honey and children gathering knowledge (147). She also makes an analogy between bees serving their queen and men of England serving their king. This is the only book considered here which so much as mentions patriotism. Rousseau does not mention it, nor does he make analogies between the action of insects and that of humans.

Mrs. Trimmer often uses learning by experience, Rousseau's method. Harriet Benson, eleven years old, goes with her mother to the home of Mrs. Addis (97-106), where she sees for herself that affection for animals can be carried too far. The kindness is no longer kindness, for the animals are unhappy caged or playing the role of children; at the same time the Addis children are very unhappy because their place in their mother's affection has been taken by animals. Another time that Mrs. Trimmer uses experience for a teacher occurs when Mrs. Benson takes both her children--Harriet and Frederick--to the Wilson farm (138-74). Here the children see kindness to animals and learn much about birds, fowls, farm animals, and even domestic animals.

On several occasions, Mrs. Trimmer uses lecturing, admonishing (201), and maxim stating (149)--all techniques which Rousseau strongly opposed. The mamma robin's lecture on pride (197) and Mrs. Benson's lecture on the proper place of animals in the affection of humans (68) are but two examples. Mrs. Benson says the proper treatment of animals is important, but they are not to be treated with the attention due human beings; consequently, she disapproves of the learned pig that all London is talking about. Harriet Benson, in the tradition of Emile, is curious and asks a question about pigs. Assuming the reader is as curious as Harriet, here is Mrs. Benson's description of the talents of this learned creature:

> Two alphabets of large letters on card paper were placed on the floor: one of the company was then desired to propose a word which he wished the Pig to spell. This his keeper repeated to him, and the Pig picked out every letter successively with his snout, and collected them together till the word was compleated. [sic] He was then desired to tell the hour of the day, and one of the company held a watch to him which he seemed with his little cunning eyes to examine very attentively; and having done so, picked out figures for the hour and minutes of the day. (71)

Mrs. Benson tells Harriet she feels cruelty must have been involved in teaching him.

The characters of both Mrs. Benson and the robin parents are modeled to some extent after Emile's tutor. They are all-knowing, but not ever-present. In fact, it is usually when they are not present that their children get into difficulty. Mrs. Benson differs from Emile's tutor in that she quotes the Bible (61) and refers to God's plan for humans and for animals (203-204). The father bird differs from Emile's tutor in his admonishing his little birds on his final parting from them "to use industry, avoid contention, cultivate peace, and be contented with your condition" (201).

The other characters in the story show little influence by Rousseau. Two of the children go to boarding schools: Master Addis and Edward Jenkins. Master Addis, twelve years old, is sent to boarding school primarily because he is cruel to animals. Edward Jenkins, eleven years old, is sent to a private academy. Although he is not sent because of his cruelty, he is cruel to animals. He recites to the Benson children a list of his heartless actions toward animals, including taking about a hundred birds' eggs, blowing out the insides, running a thread through them, and giving them to his sister Lucy for curiosities (58); he also tries to make cats fly by attaching bladders to each side of their necks and throwing them from an upstairs window (62). Boarding school seems to be the place for bad boys such as Edward Jenkins and Master Addis.

Rousseau possibly influenced the plot because there are several crime-punishment episodes, as well as the excursion to the Addis home and to the Wilson farm where the children learn by experience. Farmer Wilson relates one example of punishment suiting the crime; he says that his brother was never industrious and he eventually lost his farm and his animals and now relies on Farmer Wilson to take care of him (171). A more vivid example is the permanent lameness of Robin, the oldest of the four young redbreasts. Robin refuses to follow his father's advice on how to get airborne the first time he leaves the nest (88) with the result that he falls and bruises his wing and cannot fly for awhile (93). Later he is humble and repentant (110), but by the end of the story he can make only short flights. His punishment, however, is not as severe as that which befalls a young chaffinch who disobeys his mother and gets killed (130).

In contrast to Rousseau's idea about needless reward, Mrs. Trimmer gives many rewards to her good children and to her good birds. On one occasion Dicky gets a worm from his father for being good (27). The best examples of reward occur at the end of the story when Mrs. Trimmer devotes the last six pages of her book to stating what happened to each of the characters. The Benson children get their reward (208), as does the Wilson family (209). Pecksy, the youngest and best behaved of the redbreasts, gets hers also (213). In addition there are unhappy endings for the Addis family and for Edward Jenkins (209-11). Edward's sister, Lucy, reformed because of Mrs. Benson's lectures, so she is also rewarded (208).

There are many subjects which Mrs. Trimmer includes that basically follow Rousseau's thinking. For example, Mrs. Trimmer stresses neatness both for the birds and the children (33, 157). Rousseau and Mrs. Trimmer emphasize the importance of exercise (79); both authors do not indulge unnecessary fear of animals (49, 89, 165, 211); both stress the role of parents in the education of their children. Pecksy says, for example, that they are lucky to have parents so willing to teach them (118). Both allow a little deceit. Mrs. Trimmer permits the father robin to lie to his former mate; when she is dying, he tells her that their little ones are safe when they are not (54).

Rousseau and Mrs. Trimmer felt everyone should be content with his station in life. Mrs. Trimmer extends "everyone" to every creature, for she reminds the birds of that fact several times (21, 190, 195). The father bird tells his nestlings not to fret if ever they are caught and put in an aviary, such as the one that he takes them to see (190). Eventually Dicky and Flapsy are caught and resolve to make the best of it (213). Luckily their mother had also warned them that many evils of life come from fretfulness and discontent and that there are fewer real than imaginary misfortunes (195). Both authors stress usefulness; the papa bird says: "Every living creature that comes into the world has something allotted to him to perform, and therefore should not stand an idle spectator of what others are doing" (81-82).

Also similar to Rousseau's ideas is Mrs. Benson's statement to Frederick that she knows he has no harmful intent (24). It was intent to harm that Rousseau felt differentiated the bad child from the good one. Both writers stress charity and generosity to the poor (106-108, 116-17).

In contrast to Rousseau, Mrs. Trimmer believes in
children reading and has Frederick read and spell when he
is only five years old (117). Also Mrs. Trimmer extends an
idea of Rousseau--that of kindness to animals. Rousseau
said specifically that Emile should be kind and should never
encourage animals to fight each others. Mrs. Trimmer agrees
but goes further by calling angling cruel, as she did in her
earlier book, and saying it "hardens the heart, and leads to
idleness" (155). She also speaks out against roasting lob-
sters alive and flaying eels (156). The extensive development of the theme of kindness to animals, which is the central theme of this book, then differs in degree from Rousseau's merely mentioning it to Emile.

Mrs. Trimmer includes a number of ideas mentioned
by other writers of children's books of this period but not
mentioned by Rousseau. For example, the birds learn not
to be tattletales (135). Dicky learns not to censure natural
deformities (133). Frederick Benson learns that what he believes is kindness to animals may not be kindness from
their point of view when his mother explains the birds would
be disturbed if he took their nest and cared for the nestlings
(39). There are several examples of greed (83, 114). One
occurs when Harriet points out the greediness of pigs; Mrs.
Benson indicates how much worse it can be in humans, especially in a little boy eating too many strawberries. Frederick blushes, and hopefully knows better next time (143).
Rousseau never mentioned revenge, for Emile never had a
desire for it; but Mrs. Trimmer has the papa bird explain
why it is wrong (84). The little birds also have to learn not
to judge by appearances (198) or be hasty in their judgment
(178-79, 184-90).

Mrs. Trimmer obviously follows Rousseau's ideas
more in The History of the Robins than in An Easy Introduction to the Knowledge of Nature; but she deviates from those
ideas at will. In fact, it is only in minor ways that she
follows Rousseau, differing with him in such major ways as
having birds tell a story and having children learn from that
story.[21] Rousseau, however, influenced her more than he did
Hannah More, and the impact of Emile was felt more on almost all the other writers considered here than on either
Sarah Trimmer or Hannah More.

Notes

1. Hereafter, reference to this work will be by its later
    and better known title, The History of the Robins.

2. Harry B. Weiss, "Hannah More's Cheap Repository
    Tracts in America," Bulletin of the New York Pub-
    lic Library, L (1946), 540.

3. Mary Alden Hopkins, Hannah More and Her Circle
    (New York: Longmans, Green and Co., 1947),
    p. 161.

4. Percival Horace Muir, English Children's Books,
    1600-1900 (New York: Praeger, 1954), p. 94,
    states these tracts were written partially for chil-
    dren. Cornelia Lynde Meigs, "Roots in the Past
    up to 1840," A Critical History of Children's Lit-
    erature: A Survey of Children's Books in English
    from Earliest Times to the Present, Prepared in
    4 pts., ed. Cornelia L. Meigs (New York: Mac-
    millan, 1953), p. 80, states that Hannah More's
    purpose was also to give children suitable reading
    material.

5. Charlotte M. Yonge, "Children's Literature of the Last
    Century," Living Age, CII (August 7, 1869), 375.

6. Hannah More, Strictures on the Modern System of
    Female Education, in The Complete Works of Han-
    nah More (2 vols.; New York: Harper and Broth-
    ers, 1856), I, 318. All future references to this
    and other works by Hannah More will have the
    specific title in the text, the volume number will
    be I, and the page numbers will be in parentheses
    in the body of the text.

7. Meigs, p. 80, agrees with this opinion.

8. Montrose J. Moses, Children's Books and Reading
    New York: Mitchell Kennerley, 1907), p. 115.

9. Muir, p. 87.

10. Elizabeth Lee, "Sarah Kirby Trimmer," Dictionary of
    National Biography, ed. Leslie Stephen and Sidney
    Lee (22 vols.; London: Oxford University Press,

1921-1922), XIX, 1158-59.

11.   Meigs, p. 77.

12.   Mary F. Thwaite, From Primer to Pleasure: An
      Introduction to the History of Children's Books in
      England, from the Invention of Printing to 1900,
      with a Chapter on Some Developments Abroad (Lon-
      don: Library Association, 1963), p. 211-12.

13.   Bess Porter Adams, About Books and Children:
      Historical Survey of Children's Literature (New
      York: Henry Holt and Co., Inc., 1953), p. 64.

14.   Yonge, p. 373.

15.   [Sarah Kirby Trimmer], An Easy Introduction to the
      Knowledge of Nature: Adapted to the Capacities
      of Children (rev. ed.; Philadelphia: American
      Sunday-School Union, 1846), p. 8. All future ref-
      erences to this work will be indicated by the page
      numbers in parentheses in the body of the text.

16.   From the "Introduction" to The History of the Robins,
      the reader learns that this governess is the chil-
      dren's mother. There is however, no internal ev-
      idence in the story to indicate that fact.

17.   See page 28 above.

18.   Gillian Elise Avery, Nineteenth Century Children:
      Heroes and Heroines in English Children's Stories,
      1780-1900 (London: Hodder and Stoughton, 1965),
      p. 38.

19.   Mrs. [Sarah Kirby] Trimmer, Fabulous Histories:
      Designed for the Amusement and Instruction of
      Young Persons (Philadelphia: Printed and Sold by
      William Gibbons, 1794), p. 40-41. All future ref-
      erences to this work will be indicated by the page
      numbers in parentheses in the body of the text.

20.   Mrs. Trimmer includes another speech admirable for
      its point of view. It is the speech of an ant whose
      home has just been destroyed (151).

21.   Rousseau allowed fables told to older children.

Chapter VIII

Conclusions

Rousseau's contribution to education lies more in the various adaptations, extensions, and revisions which the authors of children's books of this period made, than in the actual adoption of Rousseau's somewhat extreme and idealistic plan for Emile's education. That this plan did not work well in real life is evidenced by Day's failure to bring up two girls after the manner of Sophie and by Edgeworth's unsuccessful attempt to bring up his son after the manner of Emile. It was Emile, however, which caused a general reevaluation of then-current teaching methods and goals of education.

The impact of Rousseau's ideas was felt on almost every aspect of children's literature: the purpose for which the authors wrote, their teaching techniques, their characters, their plots, and the themes or subjects they treated. Actually all these writers of children's books had the same purpose--to instruct and amuse. Most emphasized the didactic, Maria Edgeworth being the main exception. In every case the author intended for children to read his books, an intention which is somewhat ironic in view of Rousseau's delayed reading program for Emile. Basically, however, the purpose of the books and the goals of Emile's tutor are identical.

Rousseau's model tutor for Emile influenced the tutor-figure, a character who is present in most of these books. Thomas Day, Maria Edgeworth, and Mary Wollstonecraft follow Rousseau's example more closely than the others. The tutors or governesses modeled after Emile's tutor have the characteristics of being all-knowing and ever-present. Rousseau should also receive some credit for the increased importance of the role of the parents in the education of their children.

There is some perceptible influence of Rousseau on the notion of the totally good child, such as Jemima Placid

and Rosamond's sister Laura. Emile was a totally good
child because he was never exposed to vice, nor did he ever
show any intent to do harm. The good child characters of
the late eighteenth century, although not isolated like Emile,
remain untouched by vice. Such writers as Thomas Day,
Dorothy Kilner, and John Aikin contrast the good child with
the bad one to make the lesson more vivid and the appeal of
the good child greater.

Rousseau did not influence the majority of the minor
characters, however, nor the most human of the major characters. Most of the minor ones are merely personifications
of good or bad as evidenced by their names coming from the
humours tradition. Very few are memorable, although Maria Edgeworth's Rosamond is an exception, as are Thomas
Day's Harry and Tommy. The latter are, however, more
memorable because of the sheer length of the story in which
they appear.

In teaching techniques, Rousseau influenced Thomas
Day and Maria Edgeworth most, as they have their children
learn by experience more than do the children of the other
authors. Most writers had to include lectures and moralizing because their primary concern was a didactic one. Hannah More and Sarah Trimmer used these techniques most,
although the Kilners and Lady Fenn did to some extent. All
of the writers set up examples to be imitated.

The plots, whether they are only a series of incidents
or not, all show Rousseau's fundamental idea of punishment
suited to the crime. Many stories are merely one situation
after another in which a child gets into trouble and has to
be punished in such a way that the reader feels the sting of
the punishment. Some writers, such as Thomas Day, Maria
Edgeworth, the Kilners, and Hannah More, extend the idea
of punishment befitting the crime to reward befitting the virtue. Rousseau, of course, felt virtue was its own reward.

Rousseau's effect on plot is evident in another way.
Rousseau felt the child should want to learn; hence the tutor
contrives situations in which the child's curiosity is aroused
and he is forced to ask questions and use prior knowledge.
Mrs. Trimmer is especially good at contriving such situations.

In addition to the child's learning what he wants to
learn, Rousseau also felt the tutor should teach the child

what he needs to know at a particular time. Most of the
authors studied here include interpolated stories from time
to time in their works as the child needs to learn a lesson.

Rousseau's greatest impact on this period of children's
books came in the numerous subjects or themes treated in
those books. Many of the virtue-vice themes are ones which
are naturally emphasized in teaching children; that is, all
writers encourage children to be honest, benevolent, generous, and industrious. Most discourage lying, cheating, fighting, and cruelty to animals. Rousseau, however, contributes
such themes and subjects as the value of exercise, learning
by experience, learning according to one's individual bent,
and letting usefulness determine both work and study.

Most writers rejected Rousseau's idea of negative education, or teaching virtue by not exposing the child to vice,
because their children were not isolated like Emile. Writers, such as Dorothy Kilner in Anecdotes of a Boarding-
School and Sarah Trimmer in The History of the Robins, actually warned their children or birds, as in the latter case,
what to expect as a means of preventing the innocent ones
from being duped. Dorothy Kilner and John Aikin both spoke
against boarding schools, although both realized they are
sometimes necessary. These authors, like Rousseau, believed that it is in society that one encounters vice and hence
that boarding schools are not as desirable as individual tutors.

Rousseau's love of nature had a pronounced effect upon children's stories written during this period. This love
of nature is evident in most of the writers' teaching their
children about botany, gardening, astronomy, metals and
ores, and even geography. The creatures of nature--large
or small, domestic or wild--deserve kind treatment. Kindness toward them is one of the main themes of this period
of children's literature, but it is not so particularly Rousseau's as is his stressing the needlessness of fearing animals or insects. Writers like Mrs. Barbauld and Mrs.
Trimmer show the same love of nature as Rousseau, but
they attribute everything good to God.

Most authors disregarded Rousseau's views of God
and religion. Almost all of them include some praise of
God; however, writers like Lady Fenn, the Kilners, and
Mary Wollstonecraft, who wrote for girls, do not actually
oppose the view of Rousseau, for he permitted religion for

girls.

Boys, according to Rousseau, were not to learn religion until they were over eighteen, but they were to learn a trade. The idea of self-sufficiency, personified in Robinson Crusoe, also had an impact on children's books. Thomas Day and Maria Edgeworth both use this theme. The education of boys is, in fact, quite different from that of girls.

Many of these writers were primarily interested in educating girls. All felt Rousseau's desire for the girls to learn needlecraft and domestic duties was important. But almost everyone, except perhaps Mrs. Barbauld, had a more enlightened view of the role of women and hence a different view toward their education. Although Mary Wollstonecraft was the only one to actively advocate women's rights, the others gave their girls more history, geography, writing, and reading than Rousseau; and most considered the role of wife to be more of a companion than a "plaything of men," to use John Aikin's phrase.

Rousseau was instrumental in the popularization of such diverse ideas as the necessity of learning to swim, the pointlessness of memorization without understanding both in one's native tongue or in a foreign language, the value of agriculture, the importance of a mother nursing her own child, the dislike of fairy stories, and the child regarded as a child.

All of these ideas appear in one or more of the writers of this period. Whether these ideas be altered, accepted, or rejected, their very presence indicates the extensiveness of Rousseau's influence.

Bibliography

Primary Sources

Aikin, John and Barbauld, Anna Laetitia. Evenings at Home;
  or, The Juvenile Budget Opened: Consisting of
  a Variety of Pieces for the Instruction and Amusement of Young Persons. Edinburgh: William P.
  Nimmo, n.d.

Barbauld, Anna Laetitia. Hymns in Prose for Children.
  4th ed. Norwich: Printed, by John Trumbull,
  1786.

_____. Lessons for Children, from Five to Six Years
  Old. Boston: S. Hall, 1800.

_____. Lessons for Children, from Two to Four Years;
  of Four Years Old; from Four to Five Years Old.
  Philadelphia: B. F. Bache, 1788.

Day, Thomas. The History of Little Jack, in A Storehouse
  of Stories. Edited by Charlotte M. Yonge. 1st
  series. London: Macmillan, 1872.

_____. The History of Sandford and Merton. Corrected
  and revised by Cecil Hartley. London: G. Routledge and Co., 1858.

Edgeworth, Maria. Moral Tales. 2 vols. London: Bald-
  win and Cradock, 1832.

_____. The Works of Maria Edgeworth. 13 vols. Bos-
  ton: Sanuel H. Parker, 1824-1826.

[Fenn, Lady Eleanor]. Cobwebs to Catch Flies: or, Dialogues in Short Sentences, Adapted to Children
  from the Age of Three to Eight Years. 2 vols.
  London: Lockwood and Co., n.d.

_____. Cobwebs to Catch Flies: or, Dialogues in

Short Sentences, Adapted to Children from the Age
of Three to Eight Years. Vol. II. London:
Printed and Sold by John Marshall and Co., n.d.

Kilner, Dorothy. The Life and Perambulation of a Mouse,
in A Storehouse of Stories. Edited by Charlotte
M. Yonge. 1st series. London: Macmillan,
1872.

_____. The Village School, in A Storehouse of Stories.
Edited by Charlotte M. Yonge. 1st series. London: Macmillan, 1872.

[Kilner, Mary Jane]. The Adventures of a Pincushion: Designed Chiefly for the Use of Young Ladies. Worcester, Mass.: Isaiah Thomas, 1788.

_____. Jemima Placid: or The Advantages of Good-
Nature, in A Storehouse of Stories. Edited by
Charlotte M. Yonge. 1st series. London: Mac-
millan, 1872.

_____. Memoirs of a Peg-Top. Worcester, Mass.:
Isaiah Thomas, 1788.

M. P. [Dorothy Kilner]. Anecdotes of a Boarding-School:
or An Antidote to the Vices of those Useful Seminaries. 2 vols. London: Printed and Sold by
John Marshall, [1790].

_____. The Life and Perambulation of a Mouse. Lon-
don: Printed for John Harris, 1828.

More, Hannah. The Complete Works of Hannah More. 2
vols. New York: Harper and Bros., 1856.

Rousseau, Jean Jacques. Emile. Translated by Barbara
Foxley with an introduction by André Boutet de
Monvel. London: Dent, 1911.

A Society of Young Ladies Under the Tuition of Mrs. Teach-
well [Lady Eleanor Fenn]. The Juvenile Tatler.
London: Printed and Sold by J. Marshall and
Co., 1789.

Teachwell, Mrs. and Her Family [Lady Eleanor Fenn]. The
164

Fairy Spectator: or The Invisible Monitor. London: Printed by and for John Marshall, 1790.

[Trimmer, Sarah Kirby]. An Easy Introduction to the Knowledge of Nature: Adapted to the Capacities of Children. Revised ed. Philadelphia: American Sunday-School Union, 1846.

Trimmer, Mrs. [Sarah Kirby]. Fabulous Histories: Designed for the Amusement and Instruction of Young Persons. Philadelphia: Printed and Sold by William Gibbons, 1794.

Wollstonecraft, Mary. Original Stories from Real Life: With Conversations, Calculated to Regulate the Affections, and Form the Mind to Truth and Goodness. London: Printed by J. Crowder for J. Johnson, 1800.

Secondary Sources

Adams, Bess Porter. About Books and Children: Historical Survey of Children's Literature. New York: Henry Holt and Co., Inc. 1953.

Aikin, Lucy. Memoir of John Aikin, M. D. with a Selection of His Miscellaneous Pieces, Biographical, Moral and Critical. Philadelphia: Abraham Small, 1824.

Arbuthnot, May H. Children and Books. Revised ed. Chicago: Scott, Foresman and Co., 1957.

Archer, R. L. (ed.). Jean Jacques Rousseau: His Educational Theories Selected from Emile, Julie and Other Writings. Woodbury, N. Y.: Barron's Educational Series, Inc., 1964.

Armytage, W. H. G. "Little Woman," Queen's Quarterly, LVI (1949), 248-57.

Avery, Gillian Elise. Nineteenth Century Children: Heroes and Heroines in English Children's Stories, 1780-1900, by G. Avery with the assistance of Angela Bull. London: Hodder and Stoughton, 1965.

165

Barbauld, Anna Laetitia. The Works of Anna Laetitia Barbauld, with a Memoir by Lucy Aikin. 2 vols. London: Longman, 1825.

Barry, Florence Valentine. A Century of Children's Books. New York: George H. Doran Co., 1923.

Broome, J. H. Rousseau: A Study of His Thought. London: Edward Arnold, 1963.

Cassirer, Ernst. The Question of Jean-Jacques Rousseau. Translated and edited by Peter J. Gay. New York: Columbia University Press, 1954.

"Children Yesterday and To-Day," Quarterly Review, CLXXXIII (1896), 374-96.

Clarke, Isabel C. Maria Edgeworth: Her Family and Friends. London: Hutchinson and Co., 1949?

Compayré, Gabriel. Jean Jacques Rousseau and Education from Nature. Translated by R. P. Jago. New York: Thomas Y. Crowell Co., 1907.

Crothers, Samuel McChord. The Pleasures of an Absentee Landlord and Other Essays. Boston: Houghton Mifflin Co., 1916.

Darton, F. J. Harvey. Children's Books in England: Five Centuries of Social Life. Cambridge at the University Press, 1932.

Dobson, Austin. "The Parent's Assistant," De Libris: Prose and Verse. New York: Macmillan, 1908.

Edgeworth, Maria and R. L. Practical Education. 3 vols. 2nd ed. London: J. Johnson, 1801.

Eliassen, R. H. "Rousseau Under the Searchlights of Modern Education," American Book Collector, XII (Summer, 1962), 9-14.

Field, Mrs. E. M. The Child and His Book. London: Wells, Gardner, Darton and Co., 1891.

"A Forgotten Children's Book," Hibbert Journal, LXIII (Autumn, 1964), 27-34.

Forgotten Tales of Long Ago. Selected by E. V. Lucas.
London: Wells, Gardner, Darton and Co., 1906.

Gardiner, Dorothy. English Girlhood at School: A Study of
Women's Education Through Twelve Centuries.
London: Oxford University Press, 1929.

Gignilliat, George Warren, Jr. The Author of Sandford and
Merton. New York: Columbia University Press,
1932.

Green, F[rederick] C[harles]. Jean-Jacques Rousseau: A
Critical Study of His Life and Writings. Cambridge: Cambridge University Press, 1955.

Hamilton, Catherine Jane. Women Writers: Their Works
and Ways. 1st series. London: Ward, Lock,
Bowden and Co., 1892.

Hazard, Paul. Books, Children, and Men. Translated by
Marguerite Mitchell. Boston: The Horn Book,
Inc., 1944.

Hendel, Charles William. Jean-Jacques Rousseau Moralist.
2 vols. London: Oxford University Press, 1934.

Hewins, Caroline M. "The History of Children's Books,"
Atlantic Monthly, LXI (January, 1888), 112-26.

Hopkins, Mary Alden. Hannah More and Her Circle. New
York: Longmans, Green and Co., 1947.

James, Philip Brutton. Children's Books of Yesterday. Edited by C. Geoffrey Holme. London: Studio,
Ltd., 1933.

Jones, Mary G. Hannah More. Cambridge, Eng.: University Press, 1952.

Josephson, Matthew. Jean-Jacques Rousseau. New York:
Harcourt, Brace and Co., 1931.

Lang, Leonora Blanche. Men, Women, and Minxes. London: Longman's, 1913.

Lee, Elizabeth. "Sarah Kirby Trimmer," Dictionary of National Biography. Edited by Leslie Stephen and Sidney Lee (22 vols.; London: Oxford University Press, 1921-1922), XIX, 1158-59.

MacGregor, Geddes. "Public Schools in the Eighteenth Century," Quarterly Review, CCLXXV (1947), 580-91.

Marchant, John. Puerilia: or, Amusements for the Young. London: Printed by the author, and sold by the booksellers in town and country, 1751.

Meigs, Cornelia Lynde. "Roots in the Past up to 1840," A Critical History of Children's Literature: A Survey of Children's Books in English from Earliest Times to the Present, Prepared in 4 pts. Edited by Cornelia L. Meigs. New York: Macmillan, 1953.

Meyer, Paul H. "The Individual and Society in Rousseau's Emile," Modern Language Quarterly, XIX (1958), 99-114.

Moore, Annie E. Literature Old and New for Children. Boston: Houghton Mifflin Co., 1934.

Morgan, Penelope E. "A Few Notes on the Production of Children's Books to 1860," Notes and Queries, CXC (March 9, 1946), 92-96; (March 23, 1946), 113-15.

Morley, John. Rousseau. 2 vols. London: Macmillan, 1915.

Moses, Montrose Jonas. Children's Books and Reading. New York: Mitchell Kennerley, 1907.

Muir, Percival Horace. English Children's Books, 1600-1900. New York: Frederick A. Praeger, 1954.

Munroe, James Phinney. The Educational Ideal: An Outline of Its Growth in Modern Times. Boston: D. C. Heath and Co., 1909.

Newby, Percy H. Maria Edgeworth. Denver: Alan Swallow, 1950.

Old-Fashioned Tales. Selected by E. V. Lucas. London: Wells, Gardner, Darton and Co. , 1905.

The Osborne Collection of Early Children's Books, 1566-1910: A Catalogue. Prepared by Judith St. John with an introduction by Edgar Osborne. Toronto, Canada: Toronto Public Library, 1958.

Pancoast, Henry S. "Forgotten Patriot, " Atlantic Monthly, XCI (June, 1903), 758-65.

Repplier, Agnes. A Happy Half-Century and Other Essays. Boston: Houghton Mifflin, 1908.

Roddier, Henri. J.-J. Rousseau en Angleterre au XVIIIe siècle: L'oeuvre et l'homme. Paris: Boivin, 1950.

Rodgers, Betsy. Georgian Chronicle: Mrs. Barbauld and Her Family. London: Methuen, 1958.

Rousseau, Jean Jacques. Minor Educational Writings. Selected and translated by William Boyd. New York: Bureau of Publications, Teachers College, Columbia University, 1962.

Salzmann, Christian Gotthilf. Elements of Morality for the Use of Children: With an Introductory Address to Parents. Translated by Mary Wollstonecraft. 2 vols. Philadelphia: Hoff and Kammerar, 1796.

Scott, S. H. The Exemplary Mr. Day, Author of Sandford and Merton: A Philosopher in Search of the Life of Virtue and of a Paragon Among Women. New York: G. P. Putnam's Sons, 1935.

Shaw, John Mackay. Childhood in Poetry: A Catalogue, with Biographical and Critical Annotations, of the Books of English and American Poets Comprising the Shaw Childhood in Poetry Collection in the Library of the Florida State University. Detroit: Gale Research Co. , 1967.

Smith, Elva Sophronia. The History of Children's Literature: A Syllabus with Selected Bibliographies. Chicago: American Library Association, 1937.

Smith, Janet Adam. Children's Illustrated Books. London: Collins, 1948.

Stevens, Alice Mertz. "Rousseau's Influence on the Educational Novel." Unpublished Master's thesis, University of Chicago, 1912.

Thwaite, Mary F. From Primer to Pleasure: An Introduction to the History of Children's Books in England, from the Invention of Printing to 1900, with a Chapter on Some Developments Abroad. London: Library Association, 1963.

Tuer, A. W. (comp.). Pages and Pictures from Forgotten Children's Books. London: Leadenhall Press, 1898-1899.

Wardle, Ralph M. Mary Wollstonecraft: A Critical Biography. Lawrence, Kansas: University of Kansas Press, 1951.

_____. "Mary Wollstonecraft, Analytical Reviewer," Publications of the Modern Language Association, LXII (1947), 1000-1009.

Warner, James H. "Addenda to the Bibliography of Eighteenth-Century English Editions of J.-J. Rousseau," Philological Quarterly, XIX (1940), 237-43.

_____. "The Basis of J.-J. Rousseau's Contemporaneous Reputation in England," Modern Language Notes, LV (1940), 270-80.

_____. "Emile in Eighteenth-Century England," Publications of the Modern Language Association, LIX (1944), 773-91.

_____. "The Reaction in Eighteenth-Century England to Rousseau's Two Discours," Publications of the Modern Language Association, XLVIII (1933), 471-87.

Weiss, Harry B. "Hannah More's Cheap Repository Tracts in America," Bulletin of the New York Public Library, L (1946), 539-49, 634-41.

Welsh, Charles. A Bookseller of the Last Century: Being Some Account of the Life of John Newbery, and of the Books He Published, with a Notice of the Later Newberys. London: Griffith, Farran, Okeden and Welsh, 1885.

Wollstonecraft, Mary. The Rights of Woman, in The Rights of Woman by Mary Wollstonecraft and The Subjection of Women by John Stuart Mill. Introduction by George E. G. Catlin. London: J. M. Dent, 1929.

Wollstonecraft, Mary. Thoughts on the Education of Daughters: With Reflections on Female Conduct, in the More Important Duties of Life. London: Printed by J. Johnson, 1787.

Yonge, Charlotte M. "Children's Literature of the Last Century," Living Age, CII (August 7, 1869), 373-80; (September 4, 1869), 612-18; and CIII (October 9, 1869), 96-102.

Index

Note: Items in the Bibliography are indexed by title and author only if they appear in the notes following each chapter. Characters in stories are not indexed; see title or author of stories. References to the notes following chapters are indicated by n̲ following page numbers.

Abbé M., 11
About Books and Children, 8, 36n , 59n, 157n
Adams, Bess Porter, 8, 36n, 37n, 59n, 157n
Adèle et Théodore, 80
Adventures of a Pincushion, The, 9, 114, 129, 133, 134, 135-137, 138, 141n
Adventures of Telemachus, The, 33
Aikin, Charles, 41, 43, 44, 45, 47, 50, 51
Aikin, Edmund, 50
Aikin, John, 9, 10, 40, 50-57, 59n, 60n, 91, 118, 121, 128, 150, 159, 160, 161
Aikin, Lucy, 36n, 40, 50, 52, 58n, 59n, 60n
"Alfred, a drama," 59n
America, 79
Anecdotes of a Boarding-School, 9, 60n, 114, 128-131, 134, 140n, 160
"Animals and Countries," 59n
Arbuthnot, May H., 8, 35n
Archer, R. L., 13, 38n, 99n
Aristotle, 39n
Author of Sandford and Merton, The, 76n, 97n
Avery, Gillian Elise, 61n, 77n, 99n, 138n, 139n, 140n, 141n, 157n

Barbauld, Anna Laetitia, 9, 10, 10-57, 58n, 59n, 61n, 62, 81, 93, 110, 115, 118, 147, 148, 149, 160, 161
Barry, Florence V., 7, 8, 36n, 38n, 59n, 77n, 98n, 99n, 106, 107, 113n, 123, 134, 139n, 140n, 141n
"Basis of J.-J. Rousseau's Contemporaneous Reputation in England, The," 37n
Beattie, James, 15

Bible, 28, 62, 108, 129, 145, 146, 150, 153
Bicknell, Mr., 64
"Birthday Present, The," 84, 85-86
Blake, William, 15, 36n, 103, 111n
bluestockings, 30
Books, Children, and Men, 8, 35n, 58n
"Boy Who Cried Wolf," 141n
Boyd, William, 11, 13, 37n
"Bracelets, The," 87
British Museum Catalogue, 37n, 139n
Brooke, Henry, 62
Buffon, 12, 148
Bunyan, John, 113n
Burke, Edmund, 15

"Canute's Reproof," 59n
Cassirer, Ernst, 38n
Catholicism, 28, 81
Catlin, George E.G., 111n
Century of Children's Books, A, 7, 36n, 77n, 98n, 113n,
  139n
Chanticleer and Reynard, 45
Cheap Repository Tracts, 10, 143, 144, 145-147
Childhood in Poetry: A Catalogue, 59n, 139n
Children and Books, 8, 35n
Children's Books and Reading, 7, 35n, 58n, 112n, 156n
Children's Books in England, 7, 35n, 59n, 77n, 98n, 112n,
  138n
"Children's Literature of the Last Century," 98n, 156n
Children's Miscellany, The, 73
"Choice of a Wife," 60n
Clarke, Isabel C., 97n
Cobwebs to Catch Flies, 9, 114, 115-118, 138n, 139n
Coleridge, 42
Compayré, Gabriel, 12, 13, 37n, 38n
Complete Works of Hannah More, The, 156n
"Compound-flowered Plants, The," 54
Confessions, The, 11, 51
Considerations on the Government of Poland, 11
"Cost of a War, The," 57
Cowper, 36n
"Creed of a Savoyard Priest, The." See Savoyard Vicar.
Critical History of Children's Literature, A, 7, 36n, 58n,
  99n, 138n, 156n
"Cruciform-flowered Plants, The," 54

Darton, F.J. Harvey, 7, 8, 35n, 36n, 59n, 60n, 77n, 97n,
  98n, 104, 112n, 115, 131, 138n, 139n, 140n

Day, Thomas, 9, 15, 40, 49, 57, 62-76, 77n, 78n, 79, 80,
   81, 97, 97n, 105, 138, 158, 159, 161
death, 49, 50, 125, 132, 133
de Genlis, Madame, 80
Deism, 28, 67
De Libris: Prose and Verse, 60n, 98n
de Monvel, André Boutet, 37n
de Roquin, Madame, 11
Descartes, 39n
de T., Madame, 11
deus ex machina, 56-57
"Dialogue on Different Stations in Life, A," 54
"Dialogues on Things to be Learned," 54
"Difference and Agreement: or Sunday Morning," 55
Dobson, Austin, 60n, 82, 98n
"Dog, The," 116
Du Contrat Social.   See Treatise on the Social Contract.

Early Lessons, 9, 80, 81-83, 84, 89, 94
Easy Introduction to the Knowledge of Nature, An, 10, 40,
   143, 147-150, 155, 157n
Edgeworth, Honora Sneyd, 81
Edgeworth, Margaret, 63
Edgeworth, Maria, 9, 10, 15, 62, 79-97, 97n, 98n, 101,
   112n, 117, 138, 158, 159, 160
Edgeworth, Richard (father), 10, 15, 40, 62, 63, 73, 79-81,
   82, 83, 84, 86, 88, 89, 97n, 98n, 158
Edgeworth, Richard (son), 62, 79
Edgeworth, Thomas Day, 97n
Edgeworthstown, Ireland, 79
Edinburgh, 88
Educational Ideal, The, 37n, 38n
Elements of Morality for the Use of Children, 103-104, 112n
Eliassen, R.H., 9, 36n
Emile, 15-30, 33-35, 40, 43, 44, 45, 46, 47, 48, 50, 55,
   63, 65, 66, 67, 68, 69, 71, 74, 75, 76, 79, 81, 86, 87,
   89, 91, 92, 93, 94, 95, 96, 101, 105, 106, 108, 109,
   110, 111, 116, 117, 118, 119, 121, 122, 126, 127, 128,
   129, 133, 136, 138, 148, 149, 152, 153, 155, 158, 159,
   160
Emile, 7, 8, 9, 10, 11, 50, 64, 68, 75, 92, 99, 101, 134,
   137, 150, 155, 158
   criticism for lack of originality, 12
   criticism for contradiction, 12-13
   18th century reception of, 14
   greatness of, 13-14
   summary of
      On Education of Children Under Five, 15-17

175

On Education from Five to Twelve, 17-22
On Education from Twelve to Fifteen, 22-25
On Education After Fifteen, 25-30
On Education of Girls and Final Steps to Manhood,
    30-35
Dr. Aikin's knowledge of, 51
Hannah More's knowledge of, 143, 144
the Kilner sisters' knowledge of, 114
Lady Fenn's knowledge of, 114
Maria Edgeworth's knowledge of, 80
Mary Wollstonecraft's knowledge of, 101, 103
Mrs. Barbauld's knowledge of, 42
Sarah Trimmer's knowledge of, 143, 147
Thomas Day's knowledge of, 62
Emile et Sophie ou les solitaires, 11, 48
"Emile in Eighteenth-Century England, " 14, 35n
England, 7, 14, 15, 76, 106, 152
English Children's Books, 1600-1900, 76n, 99n, 139n, 156n
English Girlhood at School, 8
"Eton Montem, " 87
Evenings at Home, 9, 45, 50-57, 59n, 60n, 61n, 87, 93,
    121
"Eyes and No Eyes, " 53

Fables (Aesop's), 141n
Fables (Gay's), 130, 140n
Fables (Lady Fenn's), 114, 139n
Fabulous Histories. See History of the Robins.
Fairy Spectator, The, 9, 113n, 114, 116, 118-121, 138n,
    140n, 146
"Farm-Yard, The, " 116
Fénelon, 12, 33
Fenn, Lady Eleanor, 9, 60n, 110, 113n, 114-124, 129,
    139n, 146, 159, 160
Fenn, John, 115
Fielding, Sarah, 7, 113n
"Flying-fish, The, " 59n
Fool of Quality, 62
"Foolish Mother, The, " 121, 122
"Forester, " 88-92, 94
"Forgive and Forget, " 87
Forgotten Tales of Long Ago, 59n, 141n
Fortune, 13, 26, 48
"Four Sisters, The, " 60n
"Fox and the Crow, The, " 20
Foxley, Barbara, 37n, 39n
France, 7, 10, 45, 46, 75, 95
French Revolution, 144

From Primer to Pleasure, 8, 35n, 99n, 112n, 157n

Gardiner, Dorothy, 7
Garrick, David, 143
Gay, Peter J., 38n
Geneva, 14
Georgian Chronicle: Mrs. Barbauld and Her Family, 60n
Gibbon, Edward, 15
Gignilliat, George W., Jr., 62, 63, 69, 71, 76n, 77n, 78n, 97n
"Globe Lecture, A," 51
God, 28, 48, 49, 73, 74, 104, 110, 119, 121, 129, 145, 148, 149, 150, 153, 160
Godwin, William, 15, 101, 111n, 112n
Goldsmith, Oliver, 36n
"Good French Governess, The," 88, 92-96, 117
"Good-Natured Little Boy, The," 69
"Goose and Horse, The," 59n
Governess, The, 7, 113n
"Grass Tribe, The," 54
Gray, Thomas, 15, 36n
Green, F.C., 12, 37n, 38n
Guardian of Education, The, 143, 147
Gulliver's Travels, 7

"Half-a-Crown's Worth," 55, 118
Hannah More and Her Circle, 156n
"Hannah More's Cheap Repository Tracts in America", 156n
Happy Half-Century and Other Essays, A, 112n
Harry and Lucy, 40, 62, 81
Hartley, Cecil, 77n
Hazard, Paul, 8, 35n, 58n
"History of a Surprising Cure of the Gout," 71
History of Children's Literature, The, 36n
History of Little Jack, The, 9, 63, 72, 73-76, 78n
History of Sandford and Merton, The. See Sandford and Merton.
History of the Robins, The, 10, 109, 126, 143, 147, 151-155, 156n, 157n, 160
Hopkins, Mary Alden, 156n
Hume, David, 15
humours tradition, 108, 113n, 116, 123, 131, 136, 138, 159
Hymns in Prose for Children, 9, 41, 42, 43, 47-50, 59n

"Ill-Natured Boy, The," 70, 84
Imlay, Gilbert, 111n
"Innocent Romp, The," 121, 123, 140n
"Introductory Address to Parents," 139

177

Invisible Monitor, The. See Fairy Spectator.
Ireland, 79, 80, 97n

Jago, R.P., 37n
J.-J. Rousseau en Angleterre au XVIIIe siècle, 38n
Jean-Jacques Rousseau: A Critical Study of His Life and
    Writings, 37n
Jean Jacques Rousseau and Education from Nature, 37n
Jean Jacques Rousseau: His Educational Theories. . . , 38n,
    99n
Jemima Placid, 9, 37n, 114, 133-135, 141n
Johnson, Joseph, 103, 111n
Johnson, Dr. Samuel, 84, 143
Julie. See La Nouvelle Héloïse.
Juvenile Tatler, The, 9, 60n, 114, 116, 118, 121-124, 138n,
    140n

Kilner, Dorothy, 9, 37n, 60n, 110, 114, 115, 116, 124-133,
    138, 139n, 140n, 141n, 151, 159, 160
Kilner, Mary Jane, 9, 37n, 110, 114, 115, 116, 133-138,
    139n, 141n, 142n, 159, 160
Kingsborough, Lady, 101

La Fontaine, 20
Lamb, Charles, 42, 58n
Lang, Leonora B., 11, 37n
La Nouvelle Héloïse 11, 13, 14, 38n, 51
Le Père Lamy, 12
Lee, Elizabeth, 156n
Lee, Sidney, 156n
"Leguminous Plants, The," 54
"Lesson in the Art of Distinguishing, A," 51, 59n
Lessons for Children, 9, 40, 41, 42-47, 50, 58n, 62, 81,
    113n, 115, 147, 148
Letters on Botany, 51
Life and Perambulation of a Mouse, The, 9, 114, 124-128,
    139n, 140n
Literature Old and New for Children, 60n, 98n
"Little Dog Trusty, The," 82
Locke, John, 12, 18, 19, 30, 37n, 71, 103
London, 7, 75, 152
Lovechild, Mrs., 115, 116. See also Fenn, Lady Eleanor.
Lovechild, Solomon, 139n
Lucas, E.V., 59n, 61n, 78, 84, 98n, 99n, 106, 113n, 133,
    141n
Lucretia, 63

"M.P." See Kilner, Dorothy

"Manufacture of Paper, The," 51, 59n
Marchant, John, 38n
Maria Edgeworth, 98n
Maria Edgeworth: Her Family and Friends, 97n
Marshall, John, 114
Mary Wollstonecraft: A Critical Biography, 110n, 111n, 112n,
   113n
"Mary Wollstonecraft, Analytical Reviewer," 111n
Maryland Point, 114
"Masque of Nature, The," 59n
Mecca, 28
Meigs, Cornelia L., 7, 8, 36n, 58n, 60n, 61n, 97, 99n,
   126, 138n, 140n, 141n, 156n, 157n
Memoir of John Aikin, M.D., 59n, 60n
Memoirs of a Peg-Top, 9, 114, 129, 133, 134, 137-138,
   142n
Memoirs of Mary Wollstonecraft Godwin, 112n
Memoirs of Richard Lovell Edgeworth, Esq., 97n
Men, Women and Minxes, 37n
Mill, John Stuart, 111n
Minor Educational Writings, 37n, 38n
Mitchell, Marguerite, 35n, 58n
Montague, Mrs., 41,143
Montaigne, 12
Moore, Annie E., 60n, 98n
Moral Tales, 9, 80, 88-97
More, Hannah, 10, 15, 138, 143-147, 155, 156n, 159
Morley, Lord John, 14, 38n
"Morning, The," 117
Moses, Montrose J., 7, 8, 35n, 36n, 58n, 103, 112n, 156n
Mother, Nurse, and Fairy, The, 140n
Muir, Percival H., 36n, 76n, 77n, 97, 99n, 139n, 141n,
   147, 156n
Munroe, James P., 12, 14, 37n

Newbery, John, 7, 8
Newby, Percy H., 88, 89, 98n, 99n
Nineteenth Century Children, 61n, 77n, 99n, 138n, 157n

"Of Travel," 34
Old-Fashioned Tales, 61n, 78n, 98n
"Old Poz," 87
"On Earth and Stones," 54
On Education, 10, 40
"On Emblems," 51
"On Manufactures," 51, 59n
"On Presence of Mind," 55
"On Self-Biography," 51

On the Imitative Principle, 10
"On the Oak," 54
"On the Pine and Fir Tribe," 54
"On Wine and Spirits," 54
"Orange Man, The," 82
Oratorians, 12
"Order and Disorder, a Fairy Tale," 54
Original Stories from Real Life, 10, 101, 102, 103, 104-110,
    112n, 113n
Osborne, 36n

Paine, Thomas, 111n, 144
Palgrave in Suffolk, 41, 42
Parent's Assistant, The, 9, 60n, 80, 82, 83-87, 88, 94,
    98n, 99n
Parent's Friend, The. See Parent's Assistant.
Paris, 30, 32, 62
Pelham, Mary. See Kilner, Dorothy.
"Phoenix and Dove, The," 59n
Pilgrim's Progress, 7
Plato, 12
"Power of Habit, The," 56
Practical Education, 10, 76n, 77n, 80, 88, 96, 97n
Price, 111n
"Price of Victory, The," 57
Priestly, 111n
Projet d'éducation de M. de Sainte-Marie, 10
"Prudent, Daughter, The," 121, 122-123
Puerilia, 38n
"Purple Jar, The," 82, 83

Question of Jean-Jacques Rousseau, The, 38n

Rabelais, 12
Raikes, Robert, 143
Repplier, Agnes, 112n
Reynolds, Joshua, 143
Rights of Woman, The. See Vindication of the Rights of
    Woman.
Robespierre, 95
Robinson Crusoe, 7, 23, 75, 92, 161
Roddier, Henri, 13, 38n
Rodgers, Betsy, 60n
Rome, 28
Rousseau, Jean-Jacques
    educational principles and attitudes
        negative education, 9, 13, 19, 47, 83, 87, 127, 128,
            134, 151, 159, 160

180

God, 15, 28, 50, 117, 119, 150, 160
society, 15, 27, 68, 72, 85, 90, 102, 130, 146, 160
content with station in life, 15, 73, 91, 127, 134, 136, 146, 147, 154
concept of child's Nature, 15
cold baths, 16, 64
clothing, 16, 21, 64, 71, 73, 75, 130, 134, 146, 154
nursing and role of nurse, 16, 17, 102, 109, 127, 134, 161
role of mother and father, 16, 50, 85, 86, 102, 106, 154, 158, 161
qualities of tutor, 16; role of tutor, 17-35, 43-44, 54, 56-57, 65-66, 80, 81, 86, 89, 90, 93, 102; comparison with Mrs. Mason, 105; 107, 115, 119, 121, 122, 129, 149, 153, 158, 159, 160
illness, 16
country life versus city life, 16, 19, 34, 66-67
fears of child, 17, 134, 150, 154, 160
learning language, 17, 80, 96, 115, 118, 161
memorizing a second language, 20, 41, 64, 102, 130, 161
child considered as a child, 18, 161
definition of happiness, 18
dependence and independence, 18, 34, 91, 93
indulgence of child, 18, 134
false politeness, 18, 104
reasoning, 18, 24, 87, 117
importance of learning by experience, 19, 27, 40, 43, 45, 46, 54, 66, 83, 86, 87, 90, 91, 105, 120, 126, 127, 146, 152, 159, 160
purity of child's heart, 19, 117, 146, 154, 159
punishment suited to crime and/or virtue rewarded, 19, 44, 45, 46, 56, 69, 70, 82, 83, 85, 87, 90, 94, 108, 117, 120, 126, 127, 129, 130, 131, 133, 134, 136, 138, 146, 149, 153, 154, 156
exercise, 19, 71, 74, 91, 130, 150, 154, 160
individual bent of child, 19, 92, 104, 130, 160
idea of property, 19, 69, 72, 93
lying, 19, 74
generosity and virtue, 19, 43, 45, 47, 53, 71, 85, 117, 154
geography, 20, 23, 41, 71, 74, 149, 160
history, 20, 27, 66, 71
fables and fairy tales, 20, 27, 45, 46, 54, 57, 71, 84, 108, 109, 116, 118, 124, 130, 135, 147, 151, 161
memorizing and stating morals, maxims, or lectures, 20, 44, 47, 57, 74, 82, 92, 105, 117, 123, 124, 129,

Rousseau, Jean-Jacques (Cont.)
    134, 136, 137, 145, 148, 152, 159
    geometry, 20
    astronomy, 20, 23, 44, 68, 71, 149, 160
    physics, 23, 68, 117
    reading and writing, 20, 23, 40, 69, 74, 91-92, 93,
        118, 121, 129, 155, 158
    going barefoot, 21, 73
    sleep, 21
    swimming, 21, 43, 46, 47, 161
    horseback riding, 21
    senses, 21, 81
        hearing, 22
        taste (meat), 22, 33, 43, 71, 81, 96, 134, 146,
            149
        smell, 22
        common sense, 22
    fear of dark, 21, 125, 127
    games, 21, 117
    music and musical instruments, 21, 64, 65, 117
    doctrine of usefulness, 23, 66, 69, 71, 73, 81, 83,
        85, 89, 90, 93, 148, 150, 154, 160
    child's desire to learn, 23, 46, 47, 52, 53, 69, 74,
        87, 116, 121, 159
    competition, 23, 93, 136
    money, 24
    government, 24, 34
    learning a trade or being prepared for a change in
        Fortune, 18, 24, 66, 71, 75, 89, 95, 127, 150,
        161
    passions, 25, 26, 41
    sex education, 25
    self-love, 25
    self-preservation, 25
    friendship, 26
    kindness toward others or love of humanity, 26, 70,
        73, 74, 96, 138
    vanity, 27
    fighting between men, 28, 138
    kindness toward animals, 28, 47, 72, 74, 89, 109,
        117, 127, 131, 134, 149, 152, 153, 158, 160
    religion, 28, 43, 47, 50, 69, 74, 145, 146, 150, 153,
        160, 161
    botany, gardening, and nature, 28, 43, 47, 50, 53, 57,
        66, 67, 73, 89, 102, 118, 149, 160
    marriage, 29, 35
    hunting, 29
    taste and judgment of child, 29, 81, 150

ancients versus moderns, 30
theater, 30
poetry, 30, 47, 61n, 94
duties as a citizen, 34, 57
travel, 34
liberty, 35
sound of firearms, 63
pain, 63
attitude toward servants, 80, 109, 127, 136
habits, 81, 91, 104
cunning in women, 81
obedience, 81
teaching by setting an example, 13, 104, 117, 130,
    151
importance of virtue over wealth, 127, 131
educational principles for women
role of women in society, 31
reputation, 31, 124
number of children, 31
colleges, 31
clothing and fashion, 31, 32, 33, 95, 109, 121, 134
activities for girls, 31, 32, 33, 54, 67, 109, 118,
    121, 124, 130, 134, 146, 161
self-control, 31, 124
mother as tutor, 32, 41, 51, 95, 128
governess, 16, 92, 93, 94, 105-106, 129, 148, 158
religion, 32, 95-96, 104, 110, 129
reasoning and thinking, 32, 102, 124
studies, 32, 54, 57, 65, 102, 118, 130, 136
theater, 32
description of Sophie, 33, 65, 145
external beauty, 33, 117, 120, 124
gossip, 33, 109
future husband, 33
vanity, 33, 109, 136
courtship, 33
history of his ideas on education, 10-11
ideas compared with Locke's, 12, 18, 19, 30
ideas compared with Mrs. Barbauld's, 42, 43, 46-47, 48,
    50, 55, 57, 61n, 160, 161
ideas compared with Dr. Aikin's, 51, 52, 54, 55, 57,
    60n, 61n, 159, 160
ideas compared with Day's, 65, 66, 73, 74, 76, 158,
    159, 161
comparison of Day's character Chares with Rousseau,
    66-67
influence on experiments conducted by Day, 63-64, 158
ideas compared to those of Richard and Maria Edgeworth,
    80-81 83-84, 161

Rousseau, Jean-Jacques (Cont.)
> influence on education of young Richard Edgeworth, 79-80, 158
>> ideas compared with Maria Edgeworth's, 87, 90, 91, 96, 158, 159
>> ideas compared with Mary Wollstonecraft's, 102, 104, 107, 108, 109, 110, 158, 160, 161
>> ideas compared with Lady Fenn's, 116, 117, 118, 120, 121, 122, 123-124, 159, 160
>> ideas compared with Dorothy Kilner's, 125, 127, 128, 129, 130, 131, 132, 133, 159, 160
>> ideas compared with Mary Jane Kilner's, 134, 136, 137, 138, 158, 159, 160
>> ideas compared with Hannah More's, 143, 145, 146, 147, 159
>> ideas compared with Sarah Trimmer's, 143, 147, 148, 149, 150, 151, 152, 153, 154, 155, 159, 160
>> influence of Emile, 8-9
>> reputation in England, 14-15

Rousseau (Morley's book), 38n
"Rousseau Under the Searchlight of Modern Education," 36n
"Rousseau's Influence on the Educational Novel," 99n

"S.S." See Kilner, Mary Jane.
Sacred Dramas, 145
Saint Augustine, 12
Salzmann, Rev. C.G., 103, 104, 112n
Sandford and Merton, 9, 51, 62, 63, 64-73, 75, 76, 76n, 77n, 78n, 81, 84, 93, 116
"Sarah Kirby Trimmer," 156
Savoyard Vicar, 28, 77n, 150
Shaw, John M., 36n, 59n, 139n
"Shepherd of Salisbury Plain, The," 145-147
Sidney, Sabrina, 63, 64
"Simple Susan," 84-85
Smith, Elva S., 8, 36n
Sophie, 25, 29, 30-35, 41, 53, 54, 55, 63, 64, 65, 67, 84, 86, 94, 101, 107, 108, 110, 121, 123, 124, 136, 158
"Sophron and Tigranes," 66, 71
"Spider, The," 117
Stephen, Leslie, 156n
Stevens, Alice Mertz, 87, 93, 99n
Storehouse of Stories, A., 78n, 140n, 141n
Strictures on the Modern System of Female Education, 10, 143, 144, 145, 156n
Subjection of Women, 111n
Sunday School Movement, 143, 144

Taylor, Ann and Jane, 36n
"Tea Lecture, A," 55
Teachwell, Mrs., 115, 116, 119, 121, 122, 139n, 140n.
  See also Fenn, Lady Eleanor.
Telemachus, 33
"Things by Their Right Names," 51, 59n, 60n
Thomas, Isaiah, 133
Thoughts on the Education of Daughters, 10, 101-103 111n,
  113n, 139n
Thwaite, Mary F., 8, 35n, 36n, 37n, 99n, 112n, 113n, 157n
"Transmigration of Indur, The," 53
Treatise on the Social Contract, 13, 34
"Trial," 56
Trimmer, Sarah Kirby, 10, 40, 42, 109, 116, 126, 136,
  138, 143, 147-155, 157n, 159, 160

"Umbelliferous Plants, The," 54
"Useful Play, The," 118

Village Politics, 144
Village, School, The, 9, 114, 131-133, 137, 141n
Vindication of the Rights of Woman, 101, 111n

Walpole, Horace, 15, 143
Wardle, Ralph M., 101, 110n, 111n, 112n, 113n
Warner, James H., 12, 14, 15, 35n, 37n
Warton, Joseph, 15, 143
Warton, Thomas, 143
"Wary Mother, The," 121, 123-124
"Wasp and Bee, The," 59n
"Waste Not, Want Not," 84, 87
Weiss, Harry B., 156n
Wesley, John, 15
"What Animals Are Made For," 51
"Why an Apple Falls," 51
"Why the Earth Moves Around the Sun," 51
"Wife, The," 121, 124
Wollstonecraft, Fanny (Imlay), 111n
Wollstonecraft, Mary, 10, 15, 101-110, 111n, 112n, 113n,
  116, 129, 139n, 158, 160, 161
Works of Anna Laetitia Barbauld with a Memoir by Lucy
  Aikin, The, 58n, 59n
Wurtemberg, Duke of, 11, 16, 92

Yonge, Charlotte M., 78n 98n, 140n, 141n, 144, 156n,
  157n
"Young Mouse, The," 59n